A Visual Introduction
to SQL

A Visual Introduction to SQL

J. Harvey Trimble, Jr.

David Chappell

WILEY

John Wiley & Sons

New York • Chichester • Brisbane • Toronto • Singapore

Library of Congress Cataloging in Publication Data

Trimble, John (John Harvey, Jr.)
    A Visual Introduction to SQL/J. Harvey Trimble, Jr., David Chappell
        p.   cm.
    Bibliography: p.
    ISBN 0-471-61684-2
    1. SQL (Computer operating system).   I. Chappell, David   II. Title
    QA76.73.S67C47   1989
    005.75′6–dc19

Printed in the United States of America

10 9 8 7 6 5 4 3

Contents

4   More On SELECT

5   Retrieving Data From Several Tables: Joins

6   Queries Within Queries: Subqueries

7 Creating and Destroying Tables

8 Adding, Modifying, and Deleting Records

9 Views

10 Granting and Revoking Privileges

11 Advanced Topics

A   Appendix: The Example Database

B   Appendix: List of Examples

Index

Preface

Structured Query Language (SQL) is a widely used tool for accessing data stored in relational database systems. Although a powerful and flexible language, SQL can also be complex and hard to learn. In this book, we attempt to control that complexity and reduce the difficulty of learning by providing a visual introduction to the language.

This book is intended for anyone who wishes to learn SQL. While we assume that the reader has some general familiarity with computers, we do not assume any background in database systems or computer languages in general, as we believe that none is required to learn and effectively use the language. As a result, the book is intended to be useful either as part of a course or for solo readers.

The aim of *A Visual Introduction to SQL* is to give those readers an understanding of this widely used tool. As with any other language, examples are an important path to understanding, and so this book is filled with examples. With each of those examples, however, is a picture graphically showing what that example is doing. By presenting every aspect of SQL visually, we believe this often ornery language can be made manageable.

The visual techniques used in this book are based on those originally created by Metaphor Computer Systems in Mountain View, California. The Metaphor developers not only conceived the idea, but also incorporated it into Metaphor's proprietary SQL product. This graphical approach is used with the permission of Metaphor Computer Systems under the condition that no license is given under Metaphor copyright to use its graphics in any products. To allow a complete introduction to the language, we have added several extensions to Metaphor's techniques which visually present aspects of SQL not originally supported by their approach.

Books, including this one, are produced by a larger group of people than just those listed as its authors. Our primary acknowledgement, and our largest debt, is to Judy Slein. Without her painstaking reviews and her encyclopedic knowledge both of SQL and of the rules of English grammar this text would be significantly less than it is. We are also grateful to Mark L. Gillenson of the University of Miami and Diane Heydt of Micro Macro Computers, Inc. for their helpful comments, and to Tracy Mitchell, Reading, England, for assistance in preparing the book's index. Finally, we thank everyone at Wiley who helped in the development and production of *A Visual Introduction to SQL*.

J. Harvey Trimble, Jr.
David Chappell

Great Falls, Virginia
Minneapolis, Minnesota
February, 1989

Foreword

The most subtle aspect of the design of computer facilities for ordinary users lies not in the choice of screen graphics or of command and selection techniques, but in the choice of the underlying metaphor, the user's conceptual model. When E.F. Codd and his colleagues at IBM proposed the relational model for databases, their choice of a table structure with simple rows and columns provided a superb conceptual model. Indeed, today when one tries to explain this model as a step forward in database science, many incredulous new users of computers cannot imagine a database organized in any other way.

It is the beauty of relational databases that they can be visualized by the people who use them without understanding the arcana of storage management, pointers, or hierarchies. It was for this reason that we at Metaphor Computer Systems choose the relational model for our visual data access and application development tools. We developed the graphical representation of queries used by the authors in this book in order to allow users to describe visually the results they sought from a database without any knowledge of a query language. The queries so·constructed in our system *do* produce SQL queries which are sent to a relational database, but are not seen by the user, who is frequently neither skilled nor interested in programming *per se*.

The authors have adopted the same visual notation (usefully extended for pedagogical reasons) and the same philosophy of asking the users thoroughly to specify (visually) the desired results before confronting the SQL language itself. In each example, they show the complete development of a relationally sound query before it is rendered into SQL; this excellent approach is in stark contrast to the usual theme of beginning with a statement from the SQL language, torturing it to fit the example situation, and then retroactively "diagramming" it as a form of *post hoc* documentation.

This book makes a real contribution to the development of computing for ordinary users by making SQL as understandable as the relational model itself, and thus accessible as a tool to unlock the great value of our mounds of unexploited management information.

DAVID E. LIDDLE

Chairman, Metaphor Computer Systems

Introducing SQL

1

One of the most common uses of computers is to store and retrieve information. A collection of information is called a *database*, and so software called a *database management system (DBMS)* can be used to perform this task. A typical DBMS allows its users to store, modify, and access data in an organized, efficient way.

Originally, the immediate users of a DBMS were programmers. Accessing the stored data generally required writing a program in some programming language like COBOL. While these programs were often written to present a relatively friendly interface to a non-technical human user, access to the data itself required the services of a knowledgeable programmer. Casual access to the data wasn't really practical.

Computers exist to serve their users, though, and those users weren't entirely happy with this situation. While they could access interesting data, it often required convincing a local DBMS programmer to write special software. For example, if a sales manager wanted to see the total sales last month by each of her sales people, and she wanted this information ranked in order by each sales person's length of service with the company, she had two choices: either a program already existed which allowed that information to be accessed in exactly this way, or she could convince a programmer to write such a program for her. In many cases, this was more work than it was worth, and it was always an expensive solution for one-time inquiries. As more and more users wanted easy access, this problem grew larger and larger.

Allowing users access on an ad hoc basis required giving them a language in which to express their requests. An instance of access to a database is often called a *query*, and so that language is called a query language. Many query languages exist, each developed for a particular DBMS. As is so often the case, however, the one developed by IBM has become far and away the most widely used. That query language is officially called *Structured Query Language*, but is more commonly known by its acronym: *SQL*. (To make things still more confusing, it's pronounced "sequel", as if the acronym contained vowels.) Today, SQL is a standard query language, supported by a great many database management systems.

Kinds of Database Systems

Database management systems can be characterized by the way they model data as seen by their users. In the 1970's, two approaches to modelling data and its interrelationships were widely used. One approach organized the data into a hierarchy, and so database management systems using this model were called *hierarchical* systems. A widely used example of a hierarchical system is IBM's IMS. The other approach was to allow a more general organization of the data, and thus build a *network* system. Examples of network database management systems include Cullinet's IDMS and Cincom's Total.

With both hierarchical and network systems, the direct user of the database was typically a programmer, and access to the stored information was via special calls from programming languages. The organization of these kinds of systems lends itself to fast access by specially written programs. Even today, hierarchical and network systems are widely used to support fast access to stored data by computer programs. Allowing simple ad hoc queries, however, is usually not very easy with these kinds of systems.

More recently, a third approach has appeared, one which has become the norm for 1980s database management systems. Called *relational* systems, these newer DBMSs represent data to their users as simply the contents of one or more tables. Among the best known relational products are IBM's DB2, Oracle Corporation's ORACLE, and Ashton Tate's dBASE line. With the growing popularity of relational systems and the perception by many that non-relational DBMSs are somehow inadequate, some vendors have been tempted to stretch the term "relational", applying it to systems which may not quite fit the bill. Perhaps the simplest way to think of a relational DBMS is as a system in which users see all data as the contents of one or more tables, nothing more.

One reason for the popularity of relational systems is their ability to easily support access either by computer programs or directly by human beings. While hierarchical and network systems were intended to be accessed by computer programs, relational systems lend themselves quite well to interactive query languages, whose commands can be typed directly into the machine by a user. The sales manager described above, for instance, could quickly get the answer to her question if the information were stored in a suitable relational DBMS, and if a query language, such as SQL, were available to her.

In fact, SQL was developed as a query language for relational database systems. Although it is occasionally used to access other types of systems, its primary intent is to allow easy access to data stored in relational systems. Virtually all relational systems, including those listed above, allow their users access to stored data through SQL. Together, the advent of relational systems and the wide availability of SQL allow fast answers to an assortment of very specific questions about data stored in a database.

Relational Concepts

The relational model was first put forth by E. F. Codd, a researcher in IBM's San Jose laboratories, in a paper published in 1970. As was mentioned above, the relational approach to database management has since become dominant in the industry. Along with the easy access it allows to people, a major reason for this dominance is the simple but powerful view of the data which relational systems offer their users.

Tables, Rows, and Columns

A relational database consists of a collection of *tables*. All data in the database is stored in one of these tables. Each table is a simple two-dimensional structure, made up of some number of *rows* (also called *records*) and *columns*. Each column in

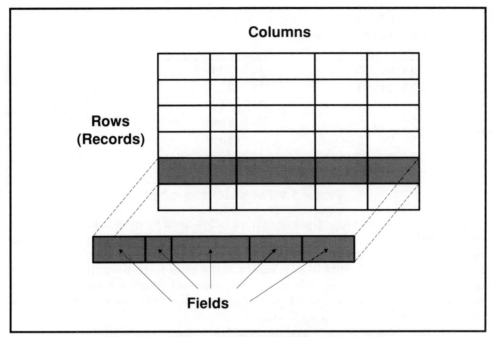

Figure 1.1 *Rows, columns, and fields in a table*

a table is assigned a unique name and contains a particular type of data such as characters or numbers. Each record (we will use this term throughout instead of row) contains a value for each of the table's columns. The intersection of the columns with each row defines the *fields* in those records.

Stored in the table, as values for the various fields in the records, is the actual data. Note that the order of the records in a table is not significant. It is not meaningful to ask if a particular record occurs before or after another. The notion of a table, with its rows and columns, is illustrated in Figure 1.1.

A very simple database might contain only one table, but most databases will contain several. For instance, the database accessed by the sales manager in her quest for the information described earlier might hold in one table the amount of each product sold by each member of her sales force. Another table in that database might contain personnel information about the salespeople, including their length of service with the company, while still other tables contain other related information. Some queries against this database, such as requesting the total sales last month by each sales person with the results ranked by length of service, may require accessing more than one table. This is not a problem, since a single SQL query can retrieve information from one or many tables within a single database. Other databases may also exist on the same system, each comprising a set of tables appropriate to its purpose.

Keys

If the records in a table are not ordered, how are we to locate specific ones? More importantly, how can we distinguish one record from another? The answer lies in specifying one or more columns in each table which define the *key* for that table's records. The information in the key field or fields must be unique for each record.

teacher#	teacher_name	phone	salary
303	Dr. Horn	257-3049	27540.00
290	Dr. Lowe	257-2390	31450.00
430	Dr. Engle	257-4621	38200.00
180	Dr. Cooke	257-8088	29560.00
560	Dr. Olsen	257-8086	31778.00
784	Dr. Scango	257-3046	32098.00

Figure 1.2 *The* TEACHERS *table*

records. The information in the key field or fields must be unique for each record. For example, in the sales database above, the table containing information about each salesperson might designate the column containing the person's name as its key. Since it's possible that two members of the sales force have the same name, however, it would probably be better to store some other value in each salesperson record, a value that is guaranteed to be unique for each. An obvious alternative is the salesperson's social security number.

For some tables, none of the information to be stored may provide an appropriate key. In these cases, it is necessary to define a column containing some kind of unique identification (typically a number) to serve as the key. For other tables, the contents of two or more columns taken together may provide the values necessary to uniquely identify each record. In tables like this, a record's key consists of its values in each of those columns.

Keys are not always required for accessing information. Depending on the question asked, it may or may not be necessary to refer to each record's key value. In spite of this, the ability to uniquely identify each record in a table is an integral part of the relational model for handling data, and every table must always define a key for its records.

Correctly selecting keys for the tables in a database is not an easy task. In fact, choosing keys is only one aspect of the much larger problem of designing a relational database. The designer, who may also be the *database administrator (DBA)* responsible for this system, must first determine how the data should be organized into tables. The best organization will depend on exactly how that data is to be accessed. The DBA (or whoever the designer is) must determine the number of columns in each table, what the names and legal contents of those columns should be, and many other specifics about the database.

Luckily, accessing the data through SQL doesn't require any specialized knowledge about how a relational database should be defined. All we need to understand is how it looks to us.

An Example Table

Figure 1.2 shows the contents of a table called **TEACHERS**. (Throughout this book, we show the names of tables in all upper case. This convention is adopted strictly for clarity; SQL in general imposes no such requirement.) This table contains six rows, each a record describing a particular teacher. The information stored about

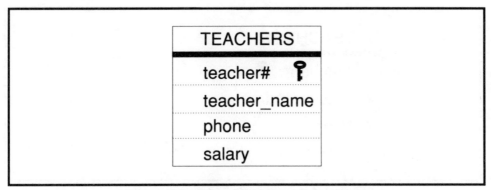

Figure 1.3 *The* TEACHERS *table, again*

each is described by the names assigned to the table's four columns: **teacher#**, **teacher_name**, **phone**, and **salary**. The **teacher#** column is designated as the key for this table.

Every record in the table has four fields, each containing a value for one of these four columns. The first record in the table, for instance, contains a value of 303 for the column called **teacher#**, 'Dr. Horn' for the column **teacher_name**, '257-3049' for the column **phone**, and 27540.00 for the last column, **salary**. Each of the other records in this table contains similar values.

The objective of SQL is to allow you to work with the information stored in a relational database's tables. Using SQL, you can create new tables, destroy existing ones, and modify a table's records. Most importantly, though, you can ask questions about the information stored in the tables, questions such as "How much money does Dr. Olsen make?" and "What is Dr. Lowe's phone number?" It is these sorts of questions which make up the bulk of SQL queries.

The Visual Approach

While SQL is a very powerful tool, it can also be rather complex to use. Among the major reasons for this are the formal nature of the language (it is, after all, still a computer language) and the inherent complexity of the queries it can express. To tame this complexity, this book (as well as at least one commercially available product) takes a visual approach. We believe that by first thinking of a query *visually*, in terms of query diagrams, you can more easily develop the formal SQL statements required to actually execute that query against a real relational database.

In the visual approach, each table is represented as a box, with each of the column names listed. Figure 1.3 shows how the **TEACHERS** table looks using this representation. (Note the little key next to **teacher#**, indicating that this column contains the key values for **TEACHERS**.) Queries about the information in a table are shown by graphically indicating the information to be retrieved. For example, Figure 1.4 is a diagram of the query "What are the names and phone numbers of all teachers earning more than $30,000 a year?". That same query expressed in SQL is:

```
SELECT teacher_name, phone
    FROM TEACHERS
    WHERE salary > 30000;
```

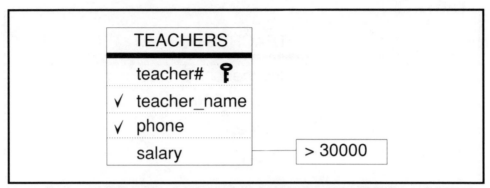

Figure 1.4 *An example of a query diagram*

For many queries, information must be retrieved from two or more tables at once. Correctly formulating these kinds of requests directly in SQL can be especially difficult. In this book, we attempt to make both these and other queries easier and more intuitive by first showing a query diagram, then presenting the actual SQL.

Someday, perhaps, a graphical interface to relational systems may be widely available. Even with today's systems, however, we can still use this visual approach to simplify the task of understanding and using SQL.

The Plan of This Book

SQL can be used to express both very simple queries and very complex ones. After describing the language's basic elements in the next chapter, we will step through a series of examples. Each of these examples begins with a statement of a problem to be solved. Next, a query diagram is shown which illustrates the solution, followed by an actual SQL query to solve the problem. Finally, each example ends with the results of executing the query.

Starting with simple queries, we will move step by step to increasingly powerful operations. By first visualizing each query, then showing the SQL and results, we believe that the query's underlying structure, and ultimately the structure of SQL itself, will be made clear.

Elements of the Language   2

SQL allows its users to work with data stored on a computer in a relational database system. Most languages for human–computer communication are rigid and formal, and SQL is no exception. We begin our discussion, then, by looking at the fundamental components which comprise this useful language.

Ways to Use SQL

In the last chapter, we briefly described the evolution of access to database systems. Starting with access by computer programs only, database systems evolved to allow direct access by people. Query languages like SQL are an essential part of this direct access.

SQL was designed with interactive access in mind. Its various commands are intended to be directly typed into computer terminals or personal computers. The results of those commands are then displayed on the display screen for the user to examine. This sort of easy interactive access to data makes SQL very effective at answering particular questions.

The need for access to data by computer programs did not go away with the arrival of SQL, however. For many applications, it is still preferable to develop software in some programming language, such as COBOL, to directly access the data stored in relational database systems. That software may, in turn, present the data to people in some form, or it may use it only for its own internal purposes. Whatever the case, direct access by computer programs to data maintained by a relational system is required.

Embedded SQL exists to make this possible. As originally defined, SQL wasn't really usable from inside a computer program. Extensions to the language have been made, however, which allow programmers to embed SQL statements in their programs. These extensions are of little interest to interactive users of SQL, and so are not described in this book. Be aware, though, that despite its original intent, SQL provides both interactive and programmatic (embedded) access to data stored in relational systems.

Versions of SQL

Natural languages have dialects. A New Yorker's English is not the same as that spoken by an Alabama native, and both differ from the English used in Nigeria. Dialects arise in large part because the users of a language are separated from each other.

SQL, too, has dialects. Originally, at least, its users were in some sense even more separated from one another than are a New Yorker and a Nigerian: they each used their own computer system. Although SQL was developed by IBM, other vendors of relational database systems quickly offered SQL on their products. And as with a natural language, these various SQL's differed from one another, as each vendor made small (or not so small) modifications and additions. The result is a potpourri of SQL versions, each implementing its own dialect.

This slightly chaotic situation is not necessarily a bad thing, especially from a vendor's point of view. If you get used to one version of SQL, then your future purchases are likely to be from the company which provides that familiar version. Once you've purchased a vendor's systems, that vendor is likely to get your future business, as well.

But many customers don't want to be tied down to just one computer vendor, no matter how good that vendor may currently appear to be. And organizations have found themselves increasingly unable to meet all their needs by buying computer systems from just one company. Instead, they wind up with a mix of systems from several vendors, each performing some part of their enterprise's computing tasks. In this environment, having several slightly different versions of *anything*, including SQL, is a problem.

The solution is obvious: standardize. Develop one version of SQL, supported by all vendors, which can be used on all systems. A standard version of the language would make life much simpler for its users (the effect on SQL *vendors* is more problematic, but at least in theory, it's the users who have the final say). In the U.S., the American National Standards Institute (ANSI) has sponsored the development of just such a SQL standard, and, based on that work, the International Organization for Standardization (ISO) has developed an internationally recognized SQL standard.

Is the problem solved, then? Unfortunately, the answer is no. First of all, the ANSI SQL standard is relatively new, and not all vendors of SQL products conform to it. More importantly, however, the standard is severely deficient in several areas. Although the standard is based primarily on IBM's SQL dialect, some aspects of SQL which are essential to full use of the language are not even mentioned. Also, the SQL standard emphasizes embedded SQL, not the interactive version. As a result, more attention is given to things which have no direct impact on interactive SQL users.

Throughout this book, we will attempt to describe a common subset of the various SQL dialects. In some cases, we will indicate where extensions to the ANSI standard exist or describe SQL alternatives implemented in different systems. If some of the examples in this book don't work on your system, check your local documentation. While SQL is the *lingua franca* for relational database access, it is not yet the Esperanto.

Defining the Language

As with any language, natural or computer, SQL is made up of several parts. Before beginning a detailed examination of the language, we need to acquire a general understanding of what these parts are and what they do.

CHARACTER	NUMERIC
DECIMAL	INTEGER
SMALLINT	FLOAT
REAL	DOUBLE PRECISION

Figure 2.1 *Standard SQL data types*

Data Types

Relational databases store data. Every element of that stored data must be of some *type*. Most generally, a type can be thought of as just a well-defined group of values. A familiar example is the type *integer*, whose values are whole numbers such as 42 and -1.

In every table, each column (and thus every field in every record) stores only data of a certain type. SQL precisely defines the types of data which can be stored in its tables. As with other parts of the langauge, however, the types supported by different SQL systems vary. Those defined in the SQL standard are listed in Figure 2.1. They are:

- **CHARACTER**: columns of this type contain strings of characters. A **CHARACTER** column has a maximum length, specified when the table is created. Each character string value contained in such a column has a length, too, which may be less than the maximum defined for that column. The abbreviation **CHAR** may also be used instead of typing out **CHARACTER**.

- **NUMERIC**: as is obvious from their name, **NUMERIC** columns contain numbers. When a table is created, its creator may specify the *precision*, i.e., the number of decimal digits which must be stored, of each **NUMERIC** column. For example, numbers up to 99,999 could be stored in a **NUMERIC(5)** column. A *scale* may also be specified, indicating a power of ten by which the value will be multiplied. A scale of 2, for instance, means that the number 5 stored in a **NUMERIC** column represents 500 ($5 * 10^2$). A scale of 0 indicates normal integer values, since $10^0 = 1$.

- **DECIMAL**: **DECIMAL** is very similar to **NUMERIC**. Once again the creator of the table may specify a precision and a scale. The difference is that with **DECIMAL**, the precision of the column is actually implementation-defined. In other words, each product which implements SQL is free to make its own decision about exactly what the precision should be. According to the standard, however, that precision must always be at least as large as that requested by the table's creator. **DECIMAL** can be abbreviated as just **DEC**.

- **INTEGER**: yet another slight variation on the **NUMERIC** theme, **INTEGER** also has a precision and a scale. This time, however, the precision is implementation-defined, and the scale is always 0. **INTEGER** can be abbreviated as just **INT**.

- **SMALLINT**: like **INTEGER**, **SMALLINT** has implementation-defined precision and a scale of 0. The only difference between the two types is that **SMALLINT**'s precision must be less than **INTEGER**'s in any given implementation. (Note that this leaves open the possibility that one system's **SMALLINT** is actually larger than another's **INTEGER**.) There is no abbreviation for **SMALLINT**.

- **FLOAT**: columns of this type contain floating point (real) numbers. (Actually, they contain approximations of floating point numbers. **FLOAT**, **REAL**, and **DOUBLE PRECISION** are all considered *approximate* numeric types, while **NUMERIC**, **DECIMAL**, **INTEGER**, and **SMALLINT** are all *exact* numeric.) A table's creator may again specify a precision for the values kept in this type of column.
- **REAL**: another type for floating point numbers, **REAL** differs from **FLOAT** in that its precision is implementation-defined.
- **DOUBLE PRECISION**: yet another type for floating point numbers, **DOUBLE PRECISION** has implementation-defined precision like **REAL**. As with **SMALLINT** and **INTEGER**, however, the precision of **REAL** must be less than that of **DOUBLE PRECISION**.

Other versions of SQL may not support the complete list defined in the SQL standard, and may allow other types not on this list. A common extension, for instance, is a type called **DATE**, intended for columns which contain dates.

One other kind of information can be stored in a record's fields: the value **NULL**. **NULL** doesn't really belong to any type, but instead represents the lack of a value. Any field of any type can have the value **NULL** assigned to it (unless **NULL**s are explicitly barred from that field when it is created; see Chapter 7). **NULL** is not the same thing as the **INTEGER** value 0, or as a **CHARACTER** value of a blank, or even as a **CHARACTER** string of zero length. **NULL** is simply **NULL**, a unique "value" indicating the absence of a normal value in a particular field.

The Structure of SQL Statements

SQL's full name, Structured Query Language, is a slight misnomer. It implies that only queries are supported, and that all a SQL user can do is ask questions about information stored in a database's tables. In fact, SQL allows its user to create tables, destroy tables, grant and revoke access to those tables, and to do several other tasks required for full use of a relational database. Although queries are its most common use, SQL is really much more than just a query language.

To allow access to the information stored in a relational database, SQL defines a number of operations, sometimes called the *verbs* of the language. Just as speakers of English rely on English verbs to indicate actions, SQL users rely on its verbs to indicate the actions to be performed on a database. Each SQL verb has a specific meaning and serves a specific purpose.

Each SQL statement, whether entered by a human being at a keyboard or embedded within some computer program, begins with a SQL verb. Following this comes further information specifying exactly what that verb should do. If the verb requests information about a table, for instance, the name of the table must appear. At the end of each statement appears a termination character. Different SQL systems define different termination characters, but the most common (and the one used throughout this book) is a semicolon.

The syntax of each SQL statement, as well as a visual approach for each, is described later in this book. For now, the important thing is to note this basic form: verb, information specifying what the verb should do, and the termination character, e.g., a semicolon. As an example, the statement to list the names of all teachers in the **TEACHERS** table is

```
SELECT teacher_name
    FROM TEACHERS;
```

The verb is **SELECT**, the termination character is the semicolon, and everything in between is a specification of what the verb should do. All SQL statements follow this same basic structure.

An important note: SQL is free-format. In other words, blanks and the line on which various parts of a statement appear are not significant. The example above could also have been stated as

```
SELECT teacher_name FROM TEACHERS;
```

or

```
SELECT
    teacher_name FROM TEACHERS;
```

and the results would have been the same.

Although conformance to the SQL standard requires support only of upper case letters, most implementations of SQL treat upper and lower case letters as equivalent. In most products which support SQL, therefore, typing the above examples in all lower case letters would have produced equivalent results.

Keywords

Like many computer languages, SQL reserves certain words for its own use. These words, called *reserved words* or *keywords*, may not be used as the name of a table, as a name for one of a table's columns, or for anything else. They always have only the meaning assigned to them by SQL. Figure 2.2 contains a list of the keywords defined in the SQL standard. As with most parts of SQL, different implementations of the language may have slightly different keywords. You should become familiar with the list of keywords defined for your system.

Throughout this book, we follow the convention of writing keywords in all upper case. Names of tables are also written in upper case. Column names, however, are always written in lower case. Since SQL is not usually case-sensitive, these distinctions serve only to make the language more readable, and have no effect on the operation of the query.

An Example Database

As described earlier, a relational database is just a collection of tables. Each table has some number of columns, and contains rows (or records) with the actual information. Each SQL query accesses the data stored in some particular database.

Throughout this book, we will use an example database with five tables. This database contains the registration information for a fictitious (and very small) university. Each table contains a related set of information, described by that table's column names. Each column contains information of a certain type, drawn from the list of possible types described earlier.

A complete list of the records stored in each table is given in Appendix A. You may wish to refer to this list while studying the examples in later chapters. For now, though, we need only see what the five tables are and what information each one contains.

ALL	AND	ANY	AS
ASC	AUTHORIZATION	AVG	BEGIN
BETWEEN	BY	CHAR	CHARACTER
CHECK	CLOSE	COBOL	COMMIT
CONTINUE	COUNT	CREATE	CURRENT
CURSOR	DEC	DECIMAL	DECLARE
DELETE	DESC	DISTINCT	DOUBLE
END	ESCAPE	EXEC	EXISTS
FETCH	FLOAT	FOR	FORTRAN
FOUND	FROM	GO	GOTO
GRANT	GROUP	HAVING	IN
INDICATOR	INSERT	INT	INTEGER
INTO	IS	LANGUAGE	LIKE
MAX	MIN	MODULE	NOT
NULL	NUMERIC	OF	ON
OPEN	OPTION	OR	ORDER
PASCAL	PLI	PRECISION	PRIVILEGES
PROCEDURE	PUBLIC	REAL	ROLLBACK
SCHEMA	SECTION	SELECT	SET
SMALLINT	SOME	SQL	SQLCODE
SQLERROR	SUM	TABLE	TO
UNION	UNIQUE	UPDATE	USER

Figure 2.2 *SQL keywords*

Figure 2.3 shows a summary of each table's columns in query diagram form. Note that, once again, one or more columns in each table have a small picture of a key beside the column name, identifying visually the columns which act as keys for that table.

The table in this database with the most columns is called **STUDENTS**. It contains information on all students currently enrolled at this university. Its columns are:

- **student#**: a **SMALLINT** containing a unique number for each student;
- **student_name**: a **CHAR(18)** containing a student's name;
- **address**: a **CHAR(30)** containing this student's street address;
- **city**: a **CHAR(20)** containing the name of this student's home city;
- **state**: a **CHAR(2)** containing the two-letter postal abbreviation of this student's home state;
- **zip**: a **CHAR(5)** containing this student's home zip code; and
- **sex**: a **CHAR(1)** containing an 'M' if this student is male, and an 'F' if the student is female.

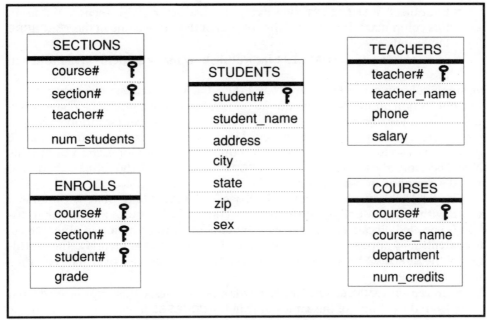

Figure 2.3 *The example database*

Because it contains a unique value for each record, the **student#** column is desig-nated as the key for this table.

Another table in the database is called **TEACHERS**. This table describes the teachers currently active at this university. Its columns are:

- **teacher#**: a **SMALLINT** containing a unique number for each teacher;
- **teacher_name**: a **CHAR(18)** containing a teacher's name;
- **phone**: a **CHAR(10)** containing this teacher's phone number; and
- **salary**: a **FLOAT** containing this teacher's annual salary.

Again, because of the column's unique values, **teacher#** is the key for this table.

A third member of the database is the **COURSES** table. **COURSES** lists informa-tion on the courses offered by the university this term and has the following columns:

- **course#**: a **SMALLINT** containing a unique number for each course;
- **course_name**: a **CHAR(20)** containing the name of a course;
- **department**: a **CHAR(16)** indicating which department offers this course; and
- **num_credits**: a **SMALLINT** indicating the number of credits this course is worth.

Because course numbers are unique, the **course#** column serves as this table's key.

Another of the database's tables is called **SECTIONS**. Many university courses are divided into two or more sections, and this table describes each section of each course. Its columns are:

- **course#**: a **SMALLINT** identifying the course of which this is a section. Values in this column are drawn from the column of the same name in the **COURSES** table;
- **section#**: a **SMALLINT** identifying a specific section of a particular course;

- **teacher#**: a **SMALLINT** identifying the instructor of this section. Values in this column are drawn from the column of the same name in the **TEACHERS** table; and
- **num_students**: a **SMALLINT** indicating how many students are enrolled in the course.

No single column in this table can act as its key. Each record describes only one section, but section numbers are not unique; several different courses may have a section 1. Also, the same course may have several sections, so course number alone is not sufficient to uniquely identify a record in the table. But taken together, a course number *and* a section number *do* provide a unique reference for each record in this table. Therefore, the key for a record in **SECTIONS** consists of the values in both that record's **course#** and **section#** fields.

The final table in this example database is the **ENROLLS** table. It contains a record with each student's grade for every section of every course in which that student is enrolled. Because its purpose is to tie together information in other tables, its contents may appear somewhat unusual at first sight. Don't worry—the usefulness of the **ENROLLS** table will become clear before the book is over. The columns in this table are:

- **course#**: a **SMALLINT** identifying a course. Values in this column are drawn from the column of the same name in the **COURSES** table;
- **section#**: a **SMALLINT** identifying a particular section of this course. Values in this column are the same as those in the **section#** column in the **SECTIONS** table;
- **student#**: a **SMALLINT** identifying a particular student from the list in the **STUDENTS** table; and
- **grade**: a **SMALLINT** indicating the student's grade in this section. A traditional four point scale is used, so a value of 4 represents an 'A', 3 a 'B', and so on.

Once again, no single column contains enough information to act as the key for this table. To uniquely identify a record, values from no less than three columns are required: **course#**, **section#**, and **student#**. Taken together, the values in these three columns comprise the unique key for each record in **ENROLLS**.

The picture of the database shown in Figure 2.3 is a useful summary of the information stored in this simple database and of the relationships between various parts of that information. Because you may wish to refer to it throughout the book, this picture is printed on the inside back cover for easy reference. One addition has been made to the back cover version of the figure: lines now connect certain columns in the tables. These lines show graphically which columns contain the same kinds of information, e.g., **student#**s, and thus can be used to "navigate" through the data. This idea is explained more fully in Chapter 5, so for now, these lines can be safely ignored.

Organization of the Examples

The bulk of this book consists of examples. We believe that the way to learn SQL is first to see examples, then to try those examples and similar problems on your system. We also believe that the visual approach can provide a clear path to understanding SQL.

Toward this end, all of the book's examples are structured the same way. Each begins with a statement of the problem: what information is desired from the database? Next comes a query diagram, showing the SQL query visually. These query diagrams are initially very simple, like the queries themselves, but their usefulness becomes increasingly apparent as the queries get more complex. By presenting the diagrams *before* the actual SQL statements, we hope to make intuitively obvious how the query should be formulated. Following each diagram comes the SQL query itself, and finally, the results of executing that query against the example database.

This organization was not chosen arbitrarily. By rigorously following this pattern, we hope to instill a methodology for approaching query development, one that is most likely to lead to the correct expression of the query in SQL.

Retrieving Data From a Table: The SELECT Statement

3

By far the most used of SQL's verbs is **SELECT**. Since the most common operation performed on a database is to examine its data, it should not be surprising that the SQL statement which does this is the workhorse of the language. In any real database, of course, other SQL statements would have to be used first to create the database's tables and fill them with records. For most SQL users, however, this task will already have been performed, and so we begin with **SELECT**. (If you wish first to create tables or add records to existing tables, skip ahead to Chapters 7 and 8.)

Selecting Specific Columns in a Table

To see the values of certain columns for all of a table's records, you must give both the names of those columns and the name of the table. The general form is

```
SELECT <column names>
   FROM <table>;
```

where **<column names>** is replaced by the names of the desired columns, separated by commas, and **<table>** is replaced by the name of a table which contains those columns. (A note on notation: throughout this book, words flanked by **<** and **>** represent generalities, and are replaced by other things in actual SQL queries.)

If you specify a column which is not defined for that table, you will get some kind of error message, depending on exactly what system you are using. Otherwise, the results of your query, a list of the desired values, will appear. To show this visually, the query diagram contains a representation of the table being queried with a check mark next to each column selected by the query.

Example: selecting specific columns from a table

• Problem

List the names of all courses, their department, and the number of credits for each.

• Query Diagram

COURSES
course#   🔑
✓ course_name
✓ department
✓ num_credits

• SQL

```
SELECT course_name, department, num_credits
    FROM COURSES;
```

• Results

course_name	department	num_credits
Western Civilization	History	3
Calculus IV	Math	4
English Composition	English	3
Compiler Writing	Computer Science	3

Example: selecting specific columns from a table

• Problem

List the names, home towns, and home states of all students.

• Query Diagram

```
┌─────────────────────────┐
│       STUDENTS          │
├─────────────────────────┤
│    student#       ♀      │
├─────────────────────────┤
│ ✓  student_name         │
├─────────────────────────┤
│    address              │
├─────────────────────────┤
│ ✓  city                 │
├─────────────────────────┤
│ ✓  state                │
├─────────────────────────┤
│    zip                  │
├─────────────────────────┤
│    sex                  │
└─────────────────────────┘
```

• SQL

```
SELECT student_name, city, state
    FROM STUDENTS;
```

• Results

student_name	city	state
Susan Powell	Haverford	PA
Bob Dawson	Newport	RI
Howard Mansfield	Vienna	VA
Susan Pugh	Hartford	CN
Joe Adams	Newark	DE
Janet Ladd	Pennsburg	PA
Bill Jones	Newport	CA
Carol Dean	Boston	MA
Allen Thomas	Chicago	IL
Val Shipp	Chicago	IL
John Anderson	New York	NY
Janet Thomas	Erie	PA

Selecting All Columns in a Table

It is often useful to see the value of every field for every record in a table. One way to do this is by listing the names of every column in that table, similar to the examples we have just seen. Because this is such a frequent operation, however, SQL provides a shorthand way to list all values in a table.

Instead of actually listing all column names, you can type an asterisk instead. The general form is

```
SELECT *
   FROM <table>;
```

where **<table>** is replaced by the name of a table. Unsurprisingly, the query diagram for this shows the table with a check by every column name.

Example: selecting all columns in a table

• Problem

List all values in the **COURSES** table.

• Query Diagram

```
┌─────────────────────────┐
│        COURSES          │
├─────────────────────────┤
│  ✓   course#        ⚷   │
│ ........................ │
│  ✓   course_name        │
│ ........................ │
│  ✓   department         │
│ ........................ │
│  ✓   num_credits        │
└─────────────────────────┘
```

• SQL

```
SELECT *
  FROM COURSES;
```

• Results

course#	course_name	department	num_credits
450	Western Civilization	History	3
730	Calculus IV	Math	4
290	English Composition	English	3
480	Compiler Writing	Computer Science	3

Example: selecting all columns in a table

• Problem

List all values in the **TEACHERS** table.

• Query Diagram

TEACHERS
✓ teacher# 🔑
✓ teacher_name
✓ phone
✓ salary

• SQL

```
SELECT *
   FROM TEACHERS;
```

• Results

teacher#	teacher_name	phone	salary
303	Dr. Horn	257-3049	27540.00
290	Dr. Lowe	257-2390	31450.00
430	Dr. Engle	256-4621	38200.00
180	Dr. Cooke	257-8088	29560.00
560	Dr. Olsen	257-8086	31778.00
784	Dr. Scango	257-3046	32098.00

Selecting Only Some of a Table's Records: The WHERE Clause

So far, every **SELECT** statement has returned at least one value for every record in the table. What if we wish to see values only for records that meet some specific criteria? To do this, we must use the **SELECT** statement's **WHERE** clause. The **WHERE** clause lets us specify a *predicate*, something that is either true or false about each record in the table. Only those records for which the predicate is true will be listed in the results.

The general form of a **SELECT** using **WHERE** is

```
SELECT <column names>
   FROM <table>
   WHERE <predicate>;
```

As before, **<column names>** and **<table>** are replaced by appropriate column and table names. **<predicate>** can be replaced by a number of different things, depending on exactly what restrictions you wish to place on the results. In the remainder of this chapter, we will examine the possible restrictions allowed by predicates.

The query diagrams for **SELECT**s with a **WHERE** clause indicate the **WHERE**'s restriction in a box attached to the restricted column. For each type of predicate, the box contains an appropriate description of the restriction applied to that column.

Comparisons in a WHERE Clause

Probably the most common predicates are those which compare values. You may wish, for instance, to see only the records in the **COURSES** table for three credit courses, or only those in the **TEACHERS** table for teachers with salaries greater than $30,000 a year. For these types of queries, the general form is

```
SELECT <column names>
   FROM <table>
   WHERE <column name> <operator> <value>;
```

As before, **<column names>** and **<table>** represent the names of the desired columns and the name of the table from which they should be drawn. The **WHERE** clause is more complex, however. The first item, **<column name>**, must name a particular column in the table. This column may or may not be among those listed in **<column names>**.

After the **<column name>** but before the **<value>** comes an **<operator>**. The possible operators are:

- **=** true if the value contained in **<column name>** equals the value given in the **WHERE** clause;
- **<>** true if the value contained in **<column name>** is *not* equal to that given in the **WHERE** clause (some systems use other symbols, such as !=, in place of **<>**);
- **<** true if the value contained in **<column name>** is less than the value given in the **WHERE** clause;
- **>** true if the value contained in **<column name>** is greater than the value given in the **WHERE** clause;

- **<=** true if the value contained in **<column name>** is less than or equal to that given in the **WHERE** clause;
- **>=** true if the value contained in **<column name>** is greater than or equal to that given in the **WHERE** clause.

The predicate ends with a **<value>**. The exact form of this value varies depending on the type of the named column. For columns of numeric types, a numeric value is simply placed after the operator. If the column is **CHARACTER** (or **CHAR**), however, the characters comprising the value must be enclosed in single quotes.

Although SQL is usually not sensitive to the difference between upper and lower case letters, case *does* make a difference for comparisons using quoted character values. For example, the character strings 'Hello' and 'HELLO' are not considered equal to one another. Also, some strings are longer than others. According to the SQL standard, comparing two strings of unequal length conceptually adds blanks to the end of the shorter string, then performs the comparison. And like numeric values, you can ask whether one character string is less than or greater than another. The comparison is performed based on the *collating sequence* used by your system. In general, this collating sequence will result in a normal alphabetic comparison, with 'A' less than 'B', 'B' less than 'C', and so on. (Whether digits are less than letters varies, though. On large IBM systems, digits are *greater* than letters, while on nearly all others, they are *less* than letters.)

In some cases, the **<value>** may also be a **<column name>**. If the **<column name>** identifies a column in **<table>**, the values in the two columns are compared for each record; only those records in which the two values satisfy the condition (e.g., **=**) are returned. Alternatively, the **<column name>** may identify a column in a *different* table. In this case, records from both tables may be examined and retrieved. Retrieving data from more than one table at a time is called a *join*, and is discussed in Chapter 5.

Example: comparisons using a WHERE clause

• Problem

List the course name, department, and number of credits for all three credit courses.

• Query Diagram

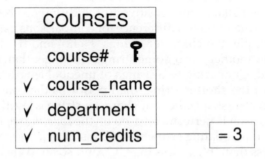

• SQL

```
SELECT course_name, department, num_credits
    FROM COURSES
    WHERE num_credits = 3;
```

• Results

course_name	department	num_credits
Western Civilization	History	3
English Composition	English	3
Compiler Writing	Computer Science	3

Example: comparisons using a WHERE clause

• Problem

List the names and salaries of teachers earning more than $30,000.

• Query Diagram

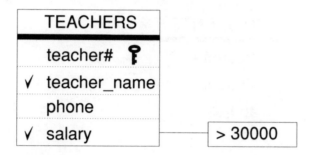

• SQL

```
SELECT teacher_name, salary
    FROM TEACHERS
    WHERE salary > 30000;
```

• Results

teacher_name	salary
Dr. Lowe	31450.00
Dr. Engle	38200.00
Dr. Olsen	31778.00
Dr. Scango	32098.00

Example: comparisons using a WHERE *clause*

• Problem

Who are all the male students?

• Query Diagram

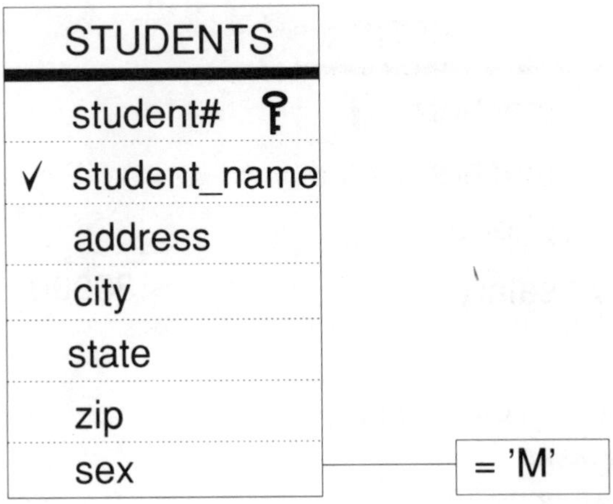

STUDENTS	
student#	🔑
✓ student_name	
address	
city	
state	
zip	
sex	——— = 'M'

• SQL

```
SELECT student_name
    FROM STUDENTS
    WHERE sex = 'M';
```

• Results

student_name

_____

Bob Dawson
Howard Mansfield
Joe Adams
Bill Jones
Allen Thomas
John Anderson

_____

Combining Predicates in a WHERE Clause

It is often useful to combine two or more predicates in a single **WHERE** clause. You may want, for example, to identify all students who both live in Chicago and are women. Doing this requires using SQL's **AND** and **OR** operators. **AND** and **OR**, together with a third operator called **NOT** are known as *boolean* operators.

Using AND

SQL uses the word **AND** in much the same way as does English. Two predicates may be combined with **AND**, and the entire predicate is true only if both of its parts are also true. If desired, either or both of the predicates may be enclosed in parentheses. We will soon see examples where parentheses are required, but for now they are optional.

Visually, **AND** is indicated by showing both conditions. If more than one condition is shown in a query diagram, you can assume that they are connected together in the actual SQL query with **AND**.

Example: using AND *in a* WHERE *clause*

• Problem

List the names and addresses of all female students from Chicago.

• Query Diagram

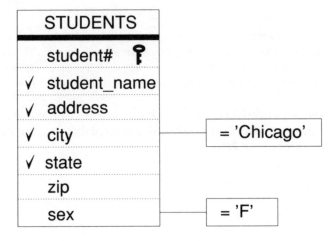

• SQL

```
SELECT student_name, address, city, state
   FROM STUDENTS
   WHERE city = 'Chicago' AND sex = 'F';
```

• Results

student_name	address	city	state
Val Shipp	238 Westport Road	Chicago	IL

Example: using AND in a WHERE clause

• Problem

Which Math courses have 3 or more credits?

• Query Diagram

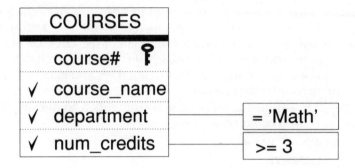

• SQL

```
SELECT course_name, department, num_credits
   FROM   COURSES
   WHERE department = 'Math' AND num_credits >= 3;
```

• Results

course_name	department	num_credits
Calculus IV	Math	4

Using OR

OR is used in a similar way to **AND**. Once again, two predicates may be combined, and the value of both is used in determining which records are returned from a table. With **AND**, both predicates had to be true for a particular record for it to be selected. With **OR**, on the other hand, a record is selected and appears in the results of the query if *either* of the predicates is true, or if both are true. Because it is used much less often than **AND**, **OR** is explicitly indicated in query diagrams.

AND and **OR** can both be used in the same **WHERE** clause. In fact, arbitrarily complex expressions can be created using various combinations of **AND** and **OR**. If both **AND** and **OR** appear in the same **WHERE** clause, all of the **AND**s are evaluated first, followed by all of the **OR**s. There is one exception to this rule: anything enclosed in parentheses will be executed first. In some cases, then, you may be required to use parentheses to correctly express what you mean.

For example, to see the names of all male students who live in either Connecticut or New York, you could type

```
SELECT student_name
   FROM STUDENTS
   WHERE (state = 'CN' OR state = 'NY') AND
         sex = 'M';
```

If the parentheses were omitted, the statement would become

```
SELECT student_name
   FROM STUDENTS
   WHERE state = 'CN' OR state = 'NY' AND
         sex = 'M';
```

It now has a quite different meaning. Since SQL first evaluates all **AND**s, it is as if the query were written

```
SELECT student_name
   FROM STUDENTS
   WHERE state = 'CN' OR
         (state = 'NY' AND sex = 'M');
```

This will select the records of all male students from New York, as well as those of *all* students, both male and female, from Connecticut. The moral is this: use parentheses whenever you combine **AND** and **OR** in a **WHERE** clause. They never hurt, and they sometimes can prevent you from inadvertently making the wrong request.

Example: using OR in a WHERE clause

• Problem

List the name, sex, city, and state for all students who are either from Connecticut or from a city called Erie.

• Query Diagram

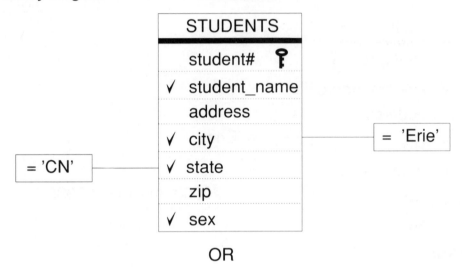

OR

• SQL

```
SELECT student_name, sex, city, state
    FROM STUDENTS
    WHERE state = 'CN' OR
          city = 'Erie';
```

• Results

student_name	sex	city	state
Susan Pugh	F	Hartford	CN
Janet Thomas	F	Erie	PA

Example: using both AND and OR in a WHERE clause

• Problem

List the names, cities, states, and zip codes of all students whose zip codes are between 20000 and 29999 or who live in a city called Erie.

• Query Diagram

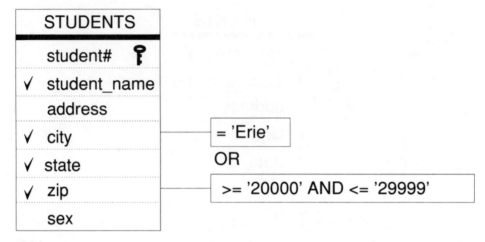

• SQL

```
SELECT student_name, city, state, zip
    FROM STUDENTS
    WHERE (zip >= '20000' AND zip <= '29999') OR
          city = 'Erie';
```

• Results

student_name	city	state	zip
Howard Mansfield	Vienna	VA	22180
Janet Thomas	Erie	PA	16510

Using NOT

SQL's final boolean operator is **NOT**. Unlike **AND** and **OR**, **NOT** isn't used to combine conditions in a **WHERE** clause. Instead, it negates a specified condition. For example, to see the names and home states of all students who are *not* from Illinois, you could type

```
SELECT student_name, state
    FROM STUDENTS
    WHERE NOT (state = 'IL');
```

Inserting the word **NOT** simply reverses the condition, returning all records in which the **state** field does not contain the value 'IL'.

Once again, the parentheses around **state = 'IL'** are not strictly required, but they are nevertheless a good idea. And although it is defined in the SQL standard, the **NOT** operator isn't available in all implementations. As with other parts of SQL, this "standard" element has not yet been completely adopted.

Example: using NOT *in a* WHERE *clause*

• *Problem*

List the names and states of all students who are not from Illinois.

• *Query Diagram*

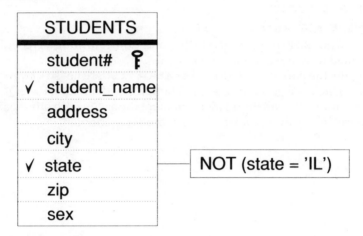

• *SQL*

```
SELECT student_name, state
    FROM STUDENTS
    WHERE NOT (state = 'IL');
```

• *Results*

student_name	state
Susan Powell	PA
Bob Dawson	RI
Howard Mansfield	VA
Susan Pugh	CN
Joe Adams	DE
Janet Ladd	PA
Bill Jones	CA
Carol Dean	MA
John Anderson	NY
Janet Thomas	PA

Other Uses of WHERE

Predicates using a **WHERE** clause can do more than just make simple comparisons. In this section, we'll look at other ways to select only certain records from a table.

BETWEEN and NOT BETWEEN

Using **>=**, **<=**, and **AND**, it is possible to select records where values of a specific field in the record fall within a specified range. In an earlier example, for instance, we listed the name and other information for all students with zip codes from 20000 to 29999. This kind of query arises quite often, and so SQL provides a shorthand way of expressing it. By using **BETWEEN** and **NOT BETWEEN** in a **WHERE** clause, we can directly specify ranges of values. The general form is

```
SELECT <column names>
    FROM <table>
    WHERE <column name> BETWEEN <value1> AND <value2>;
```
The negative form is also available, as

```
SELECT <column names>
    FROM <table>
    WHERE <column name> NOT BETWEEN <value1> AND <value2>;
```
In the first case, only those records in which the values in **<column name>** are greater than or equal to **<value1>** and less than or equal to **<value2>** will be selected. In the second, only those records whose values are *not* within the specified range will be selected. In both forms, the two values are assumed to be specified in ascending order, i.e., **<value1>** is less than **<value2>**.

For example, to see the names and salaries of all teachers who earn between $30,000 and $35,000 a year, you could type

```
SELECT teacher_name, salary
    FROM TEACHERS
    WHERE salary BETWEEN 30000 AND 35000;
```
Only those records from **TEACHERS** with salaries in the specified range will be returned.

The values specified in the **WHERE** clause can be of any type, but **<value1>** and **<value2>** must both be of a type comparable to that defined for **<column name>**. For example, the query

```
SELECT student_name
    FROM students
    WHERE student_name BETWEEN 0 AND 100;
```
is not legal, because **student_name** is a **CHAR** column, while the values **0** and **100** are numeric.

Example: *using* BETWEEN *in a* WHERE *clause*

• Problem

List the names and salaries of teachers who make between $30,000 and $35,000 a year.

• Query Diagram

• SQL

```
SELECT teacher_name, salary
    FROM TEACHERS
    WHERE salary BETWEEN 30000 AND 35000;
```

• Results

teacher_name	salary
Dr. Lowe	31450.00
Dr. Olsen	31778.00
Dr. Scango	32098.00

Example: using NOT BETWEEN *in a* WHERE *clause*

• Problem

List the names, cities, states, and zip codes of students whose zip codes are *not* between 20000 and 29999.

• Query Diagram

```
┌─────────────────────┐
│      STUDENTS       │
├─────────────────────┤
│   student#    ?     │
│ ✓ student_name      │
│   address           │
│ ✓ city              │
│ ✓ state             │
│ ✓ zip ──────────────┼──── NOT BETWEEN '20000' AND '29999'
│   sex               │
└─────────────────────┘
```

• SQL

```
SELECT student_name, city, state, zip
    FROM STUDENTS
    WHERE zip NOT BETWEEN '20000' AND '29999';
```

• Results

student_name	city	state	zip
Susan Powell	Haverford	PA	19041
Bob Dawson	Newport	RI	02891
Susan Pugh	Hartford	CN	06107
Joe Adams	Newark	DE	19702
Janet Ladd	Pennsburg	PA	18073
Bill Jones	Newport	CA	92660
Carol Dean	Boston	MA	02169
Allen Thomas	Chicago	IL	60624
Val Shipp	Chicago	IL	60556
John Anderson	New York	NY	10008
Janet Thomas	Erie	PA	16510

LIKE and NOT LIKE

When searching for information, we often already know part of what we're looking for. We may, for instance, know someone's last name but not their first name, or we may know only that their last name begins with "Jo". For situations like these, SQL provides **LIKE** and **NOT LIKE**. The general form of a **SELECT** using **LIKE** is

    SELECT <column names>
        FROM <table>
        WHERE <column name> LIKE <value>;

The form with **NOT LIKE** is similar.

    SELECT <column names>
        FROM <table>
        WHERE <column name> NOT LIKE <value>;

LIKE and **NOT LIKE** may only be used with character columns. **<column name>**, therefore, must identify a **CHAR** column, and **<value>** must be a character string enclosed in single quotes.

In the simplest case, **LIKE** and **NOT LIKE** function like = and <>. So, for example, the statement

    SELECT teacher#
        FROM TEACHERS
        WHERE teacher_name LIKE 'Dr. Engle';

is equivalent to saying

    SELECT teacher#
        FROM TEACHERS
        WHERE teacher_name = 'Dr. Engle';

The power of these two operators is based on defining two special wild card characters: a percent sign (%) and an underscore (_). When contained within the quoted character string value, a percent sign matches any string of characters, of any length. An underscore, on the other hand, matches any single character. Using these two wild cards, a wide variety of searches can be performed.

The **WHERE** clause in the example above would also have returned information about Dr. Engle's record if it had read **WHERE teacher_name LIKE 'Dr. %'**. In this case, however, it would have returned information about other records in the TEACHERS table, too. To further limit the records returned, we could have said **WHERE teacher_name LIKE 'Dr. %e'**. This would have returned records for all teachers with the title 'Dr.' and whose name ends in a lower case 'e' (recall that the difference between upper and lower case letters is significant inside quoted strings). We could also have said **WHERE teacher_name LIKE 'Dr. E_ _ _e'**. This would return information about teachers whose last names begin with 'E', end with 'e', and have three letters (any three letters) in between.

Since **LIKE** returns records with fields that match a specified string (possibly with embedded wild card characters), **NOT LIKE** does just the opposite: it returns all records where the specified field does *not* match the string. For example, the SQL statement

```
SELECT teacher#
    FROM TEACHERS
    WHERE teacher_name NOT LIKE 'Dr. Engle';
```
would return the teacher number for every teacher *except* Dr. Engle.

Example: *using* LIKE *in a* WHERE *clause*

• Problem

List the name and sex of every student whose name begins with "Jo".

• Query Diagram

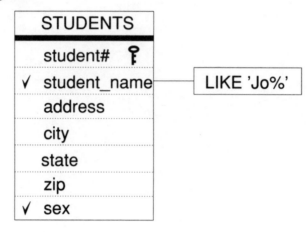

• SQL

```
SELECT student_name, sex
    FROM STUDENTS
    WHERE student_name LIKE 'Jo%';
```

• Results

student_name	sex
Joe Adams	M
John Anderson	M

Example: *using* LIKE *in a* WHERE *clause*

• Problem

List the names and home states of all students from states that begin with the letter 'C'.

• Query Diagram

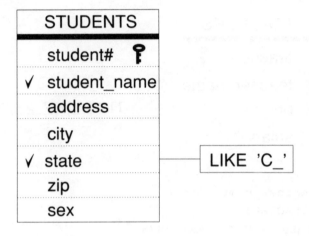

• SQL

```
SELECT student_name, state
   FROM STUDENTS
   WHERE state LIKE 'C_';
```

• Results

student_name	state
Susan Pugh	CN
Bill Jones	CA

Example: *using* NOT LIKE *in a* WHERE *clause*

• Problem

List the names and phone numbers of all teachers whose phone numbers do *not* begin with 257.

• Query Diagram

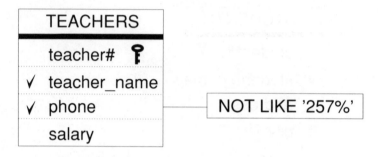

• SQL

```
SELECT teacher_name, phone
    FROM TEACHERS
    WHERE phone NOT LIKE '257%';
```

• Results

teacher_name	phone
Dr. Engle	256-4621

IN and NOT IN

Another possible way to restrict which records are selected is to use **IN** and **NOT IN**. Like the other mechanisms discussed so far, they appear in the **WHERE** clause, and only records that match their requirements are returned. The general form of a SQL statement using **IN** is

```
SELECT <column names>
    FROM <table>
    WHERE <column name> IN (<values>);
```

The form with **NOT IN** is

```
SELECT <column names>
    FROM <table>
    WHERE <column name> NOT IN (<values>);
```

In both cases, **(<values>)** consists of one or more values, separated by commas and enclosed in parentheses, all of a type comparable to that of the column identified by **<column name>**. In other words, if **<column name>** is a **CHAR** column, the values must all be quoted character strings. If **<column name>** identifies a numeric column, such as **INTEGER** or **SMALLINT**, then the values must also be numbers. For **IN**, the records returned are those where the field named **<column name>** contains one of the values specified in the parenthesized list. For **NOT IN**, the reverse is true: the records returned are those whose **<column name>** field does not contain any of the values in the list.

Using **IN** is equivalent to grouping several tests for equality together with ORs. This is yet another example of a shorthand form provided by SQL for common requests. For example, the statement

```
SELECT course_name, department
    FROM COURSES
    WHERE department IN ('Math','English');
```

will return all records where the **department** field contains either **'Math'** or **'English'**. This is equivalent to saying

```
SELECT course_name, department
    FROM COURSES
    WHERE department = 'Math' OR
          department = 'English';
```

Similarly, **NOT IN** is equivalent to grouping tests for inequality together with ANDs. The statement

```
SELECT course_name, department
    FROM COURSES
    WHERE department NOT IN ('Math','English');
```

is equivalent to

```
SELECT course_name, department
    FROM COURSES
    WHERE department <> 'Math' AND
          department <> 'English';
```

Example: using IN in a WHERE clause

• Problem

List the names and departments of all Math and English courses.

• Query Diagram

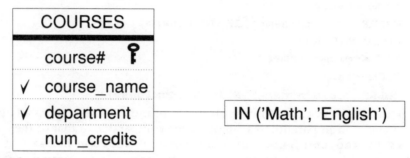

• SQL

```
SELECT course_name, department
    FROM COURSES
    WHERE department IN ('Math','English');
```

• Results

course_name	department
Calculus IV	Math
English Composition	English

Example: using NOT IN *in a* WHERE *clause*

• Problem

List the names, cities, and states of all students who are *not* from California or Illinois.

• Query Diagram

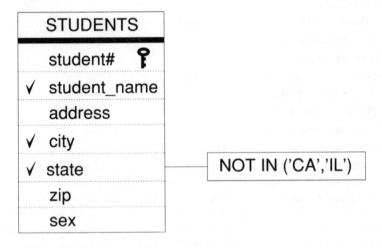

• SQL

```
SELECT student_name, city, state
    FROM STUDENTS
    WHERE state NOT IN ('CA','IL');
```

• Results

student_name	city	state
Susan Powell	Haverford	PA
Bob Dawson	Newport	RI
Howard Mansfield	Vienna	VA
Susan Pugh	Hartford	CN
Joe Adams	Newark	DE
Janet Ladd	Pennsburg	PA
Carol Dean	Boston	MA
John Anderson	New York	NY
Janet Thomas	Erie	PA

IS NULL and IS NOT NULL

In the last chapter, we described the special value **NULL**. Unlike **CHAR** or numeric values, which can only be assigned to **CHAR** or numeric fields, respectively, the value **NULL** can be assigned to any field, regardless of its type. **NULL** is different from other values as well in that it can't be used in simple comparisons. A **WHERE** clause using the = operator to ask whether some field is **NULL** is undefined; it is neither true nor false. Instead, the special constructions **IS NULL** and **IS NOT NULL** must be used.

The general form of a **SELECT** statement with **IS NULL** is

    SELECT <column names>

      FROM <table>

      WHERE <column name> IS NULL;

For one using **IS NOT NULL**, the form is

    SELECT <column names>

      FROM <table>

      WHERE <column name> IS NOT NULL;

Like all **WHERE** clauses, these two select only records that meet their requirements. A query with **IS NULL** will return only those records in which the field identified by **<column name>** contains the value **NULL**, while those with **IS NOT NULL** will return only those in which **<column name>** contains a value other than **NULL**. The **IS NULL** construction is the only way to search for records containing the value **NULL**. **BETWEEN**, **LIKE**, and the other **WHERE** clause options can never find **NULL** values.

Example: using IS NULL in a WHERE clause

• Problem

List the entire contents of any records in the **ENROLLS** table with a **NULL** value for grade.

• Query Diagram

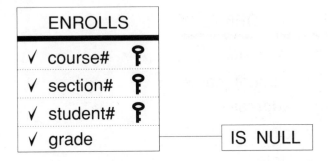

• SQL

```
SELECT *
    FROM ENROLLS
    WHERE grade IS NULL;
```

• Results

course#	section#	student#	grade
450	2	548	

• Note

Because **NULL** really means "no value", representing it in query results is problematic. We use blanks to indicate a **NULL**, but different implementations of SQL use different representations. Some even allow their users to choose how **NULL** values are represented in query results.

Example: *using* IS NOT NULL *in a* WHERE *clause*

• Problem

List the names, cities, states, and zip codes for all students whose zip codes are not **NULL**.

• Query Diagram

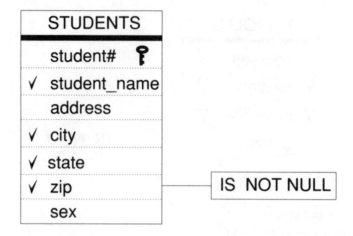

• SQL

```
SELECT student_name, city, state, zip
    FROM STUDENTS
    WHERE zip IS NOT NULL;
```

• Results

student_name	city	state	zip
Susan Powell	Haverford	PA	19041
Bob Dawson	Newport	RI	02891
Howard Mansfield	Vienna	VA	22180
Susan Pugh	Hartford	CN	06107
Joe Adams	Newark	DE	19702
Janet Ladd	Pennsburg	PA	18073
Bill Jones	Newport	CA	92660
Carol Dean	Boston	MA	02169
Allen Thomas	Chicago	IL	60624
Val Shipp	Chicago	IL	60556
John Anderson	New York	NY	10008
Janet Thomas	Erie	PA	16510

More On SELECT

4

So far, we've seen several ways to use the **SELECT** statement to retrieve all or part of a table's data. In this chapter, we will see how that data can be ordered, grouped, or otherwise manipulated while it is being retrieved.

Ordering Selected Data

Recall that the order of the records within a table has no significance to SQL. When records are retrieved from a table, therefore, the order in which they appear is arbitrary. Sometimes, we wish to see the data resulting from a query ordered in a specific way. To allow this, SQL provides the **ORDER BY** option for the **SELECT** statement.

The general form of a **SELECT** statement using **ORDER BY** is

```
SELECT <column names>
    FROM <table>
    <WHERE clause>
    ORDER BY <column names>;
```

As before, **<column names>** after **SELECT** and **<table>** indicate the columns which should be selected from the named table. A **<WHERE clause>** may option-ally appear, specifying conditions which records must meet to be selected. Most im-portantly for our purposes, the **<column names>** following **ORDER BY** indicate the column or columns whose values should be used to order the selected records. For example, the statement

```
SELECT teacher_name, salary
    FROM TEACHERS
    ORDER BY teacher_name;
```

will produce an alphabetical list of all teachers. Note that the columns specified after **ORDER BY** must be drawn from those following **SELECT** in the query.

Results may also be ordered by more than one column. Saying

```
SELECT student_name, city, state
    FROM STUDENTS
    ORDER BY state, student_name;
```

will yield a list of students ordered first by state, then alphabetically by name within each state.

One more possibility: instead of giving the name of a column by which to order selected records, it is possible to give a column's number. Column numbers refer to columns in the *results* of the query, not in the original table, and go from left to right, beginning with one. This means, for instance, that the first example shown above could also have been expressed as

```
SELECT teacher_name, salary
    FROM TEACHERS
    ORDER BY 1;
```

The results would have been exactly the same, because **teacher_name** is the first column from the left in the results of this query.

SQL also allows records to be listed in reverse order. Suppose, for example, that we wished for some reason to see a list of teachers and their salaries in reverse alphabetical order. We could use the **DESC** option with **ORDER BY**:

```
SELECT teacher_name, salary
    FROM TEACHERS
    ORDER BY teacher_name DESC;
```

It's hard to see why it would be useful, but it is also legal to replace **DESC** with **ASC**. This causes the results to be listed in ascending order, just as if neither **ASC** nor **DESC** were specified.

The query diagram for **ORDER BY** is very much like the one for **WHERE** clauses. It shows the selected table with a box indicating the column on which the ordering is to be based. If two or more columns are used, both are included in the **ORDER BY** box.

Example: listing selected data in order using column name

• Problem

Give an alphabetical list of teachers and their phone numbers.

• Query Diagram

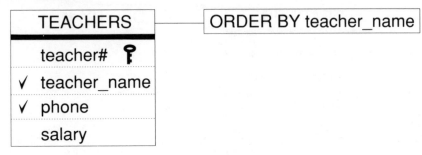

• SQL

```
SELECT teacher_name, phone
    FROM TEACHERS
    ORDER BY teacher_name;
```

• Results

teacher_name	phone
Dr. Cooke	257-8088
Dr. Engle	256-4621
Dr. Horn	257-3049
Dr. Lowe	257-2390
Dr. Olsen	257-8086
Dr. Scango	257-3046

Example: listing selected data in order using column number

• Problem

Give an alphabetical list of teachers and their phone numbers.

• Query Diagram

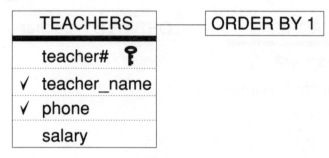

• SQL

```
SELECT teacher_name, phone
    FROM TEACHERS
    ORDER BY 1;
```

• Results

teacher_name	phone
Dr. Cooke	257-8088
Dr. Engle	256-4621
Dr. Horn	257-3049
Dr. Lowe	257-2390
Dr. Olsen	257-8086
Dr. Scango	257-3046

Example: listing selected data in reverse order

• *Problem*

Give a list of teachers and their phone numbers in reverse alphabetical order.

• *Query Diagram*

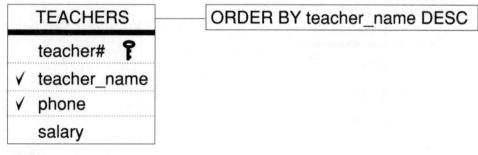

• *SQL*

```
SELECT teacher_name, phone
    FROM TEACHERS
    ORDER BY teacher_name DESC;
```

• *Results*

teacher_name	phone
Dr. Scango	257-3046
Dr. Olsen	257-8086
Dr. Lowe	257-2390
Dr. Horn	257-3049
Dr. Engle	256-4621
Dr. Cooke	257-8088

Example: ordering selected data by two columns

• Problem

List the names, cities, and states of all students ordered first by state, then by city within that state.

• Query Diagram

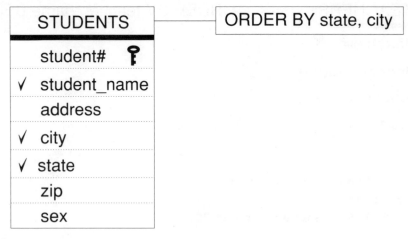

• SQL

```
SELECT student_name, city, state
    FROM STUDENTS
    ORDER BY state, city;
```

• Results

student_name	city	state
Bill Jones	Newport	CA
Susan Pugh	Hartford	CN
Joe Adams	Newark	DE
Allen Thomas	Chicago	IL
Val Shipp	Chicago	IL
Carol Dean	Boston	MA
John Anderson	New York	NY
Janet Thomas	Erie	PA
Susan Powell	Haverford	PA
Janet Ladd	Pennsburg	PA
Bob Dawson	Newport	RI
Howard Mansfield	Vienna	VA

Example: combining ordering with a WHERE *clause*

• Problem

List all three credit courses alphabetically by department.

• Query Diagram

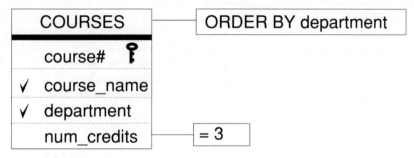

• SQL

```
SELECT department, course_name
    FROM COURSES
    WHERE num_credits = 3
    ORDER BY department;
```

• Results

department	course_name
Computer Science	Compiler Writing
English	English Composition
History	Western Civilization

Doing Arithmetic With Selected Information

Retrieving the information stored in a table is undoubtedly useful. Sometimes, though, the stored information is not exactly what we're interested in. Suppose, for example, that we wish to know how much each teacher's salary would be if we gave everyone a flat $1,000 raise. Or perhaps we'd like to compare this with what the new salaries would be after an across-the-board 10 percent increase. For these kinds of queries, SQL provides the four basic arithmetic operations of addition, subtraction, multiplication, and division. (While addition and subtraction are represented in queries by the familiar + and − symbols, multiplication and division use the symbols * and /, respectively.) Within a query, for instance, we can add a fixed amount to every value in a column, or multiply each of a column's values by some amount. It is even possible to add two columns together or subtract the values of one column in a record from those of another.

To see what each teacher's salary would be after a flat $1,000 raise, you could type

```
SELECT teacher_name, new_salary = salary + 1000
    FROM TEACHERS;
```

Because the second column of the results will be derived from one of the table's original columns, we give it a new name by adding **new_salary =** in front of the arithmetic expression. In the results table, that column now will be labelled with our new name. If you had not specified this new name, the name assigned to the newly created column would depend on your particular implementation of SQL.

Similarly, to see what the teachers' salaries would be after a 10 percent raise, the query is

```
SELECT teacher_name, new_salary = salary * 1.10
    FROM TEACHERS;
```

As usual, a **WHERE** clause can be added to the query to restrict which records are selected. To see, for example, the results of giving a 10 percent raise only to those teachers earning less than $30,000, one could type

```
SELECT teacher_name, new_salary = salary * 1.10
    FROM TEACHERS
    WHERE salary < 30000;
```

As might be expected, these arithmetic operations can only be used on columns containing numeric values. The query diagrams for queries containing these "derived columns" temporarily add an extra field to the table from which the values are derived.

Also, the four operations can be combined to form arbitrarily complex expressions. When two or more operations are combined in a single query, SQL defines rules for the *precedence* of each. In general, all occurrences of * and /, multiplication and division, are performed first, followed by all occurrences of + and −, addition and subtraction. Operations of equal precedence are carried out left to right.

If desired, these rules can be overridden by using parentheses: anything inside parentheses happens first. For example, the expression

```
salary - 10 + 5
```

would first subtract 10 from salary, then add 5 back (*why* you would want to do this is unclear, but it's only an example). If we change the + to a *, however, giving

```
salary - 10 * 5
```

the precedence rules described above cause a quite different outcome. Because multiplication has higher precedence than subtraction, the 10 * 5 happens first, and so **salary** is reduced by 50. If we instead wanted to subtract 10 from **salary**, then multiply the result by 5, we would need parentheses:

```
(salary - 10) * 5
```

With the added parentheses, the subtraction is performed first, followed by the multiplication.

What about **NULL** values? Recall from Chapter 2 that a **NULL** in a numeric field isn't the same as a 0, but is instead a value unique to itself. How then are **NULL**s handled during arithmetic operations?

The rule turns out to be somewhat extreme, but very simple: any arithmetic operation applied to a column containing a **NULL** value in one of its fields will return the value **NULL**. This means, for instance, that for any record in the **TEACHERS** table which contains a **NULL** in its **salary** field, every expression involving that record's **salary** will also result in the value **NULL**.

This simple but inflexible rule can sometimes be rather limiting. To avoid the problems of **NULL** values, it is possible to specify during a table's creation that one or more of its columns may not contain **NULL**s. Chapter 7 describes how to place this useful restriction on new tables.

Example: using arithmetic operations in queries

• Problem

What would each teacher's salary be if he or she received a 5.5 percent cost of living increase and a $1,500 merit increase?

• Query Diagram

```
┌─────────────────────────────┐
│         TEACHERS            │
├─────────────────────────────┤
│    teacher#   ?             │
│ ✓  teacher_name             │
│    phone                    │
│    salary                   │
└─────────────────────────────┘
  ✓   new_salary = (salary * 1.055) + 1500
```

• SQL

```
SELECT teacher_name,
       new_salary = (salary * 1.055) + 1500
   FROM TEACHERS;
```

• Results

teacher_name	new_salary
Dr. Horn	30554.70
Dr. Lowe	34679.75
Dr. Engle	41801.00
Dr. Cooke	32685.80
Dr. Olsen	35025.79
Dr. Scango	35363.39

Using Aggregates

SQL provides a number of built-in functions for performing common operations. These functions, called "set functions" by the SQL standard but more often referred to as *aggregates*, make it easy for us to find the maximum or minimum value in a column, find the sum or average of a column's values, and count the number of records in a table. While all of these things would be possible without them, SQL's aggregates make the task much simpler.

Finding Maximum and Minimum Values

It is often interesting to ask about the limits of data values stored in a table. Which teacher makes the most money? Which student received the lowest grade? For answering questions like these, SQL provides the **MAX** and **MIN** aggregates.

Both **MAX** and **MIN** can be used like the name of a column in a **SELECT**. You could type, for example,

```
SELECT MAX(salary)
    FROM TEACHERS;
```

or

```
SELECT MIN(grade)
    FROM ENROLLS;
```

The first query would select and display the maximum value from the **salary** column of the **TEACHERS** table, while the second would display the minimum value from the **grade** column of the **ENROLLS** table. The name of the query's result defaults to, for example, **MAX(salary)**. A different name can be assigned, if desired, through the mechanism seen earlier, e.g.,

```
SELECT maximum = MAX(salary)
    FROM TEACHERS;
```

(It's worth noting that both the default name assigned to the query's result and the exact syntax used to change that default name may vary from one implementation of SQL to another.)

It is also possible to use a **WHERE** clause to select the maximum or minimum value from a group of records meeting some specified criteria. We could, for example, say

```
SELECT MAX(salary)
    FROM TEACHERS
    WHERE teacher# > 300;
```

This query selects the largest salary only from those records in the **TEACHERS** table that have a **teacher#** greater than 300.

What if, instead of the query using **MAX** above, you wanted to know not only what the maximum teacher salary was, but also who earned it? You might have naively typed

```
SELECT teacher_name, MAX(salary)
    FROM TEACHERS;
```

Unfortunately, you would have received an error message from SQL, as the above query is illegal. It's illegal because, in simple cases such as this, SQL requires that a query return the same number of values for every column name specified. Thus far, this has not been a problem, since each table has the same number of values in each of its columns.

When using **MAX** and **MIN**, however, the situation changes. As mentioned above, **MAX** and **MIN** function somewhat like column names, and yet by their nature, both always return only a single value. Because of SQL's rule that queries must always return the same number of values for each specified column name, no other column names (except for those appearing within other aggregates) can be specified along with **MAX** or **MIN**. As we shall see, all SQL aggregates share this same limitation. (There is one significant exception: using **GROUP BY**, described at the end of this chapter, allows other column names to appear in a **SELECT** along with **MAX**, **MIN**, and other aggregates.)

Although they probably make the most sense when used with numeric columns, **MAX** and **MIN** can also be used with character columns. With character columns, it is as if all the values in the column are first placed in alphabetical order, then the last value (for **MAX**) or the first value (for **MIN**) is returned.

As was the case with arithmetic operations, we must once more ask: what about **NULL**s? Unlike the arithmetic operators, all of which return **NULL** if *any* of a column's values are **NULL**, **MAX** and **MIN** *ignore* **NULL** values. This makes some sense, since it's hard to see how **NULL** could be compared to other values in a particular column.

All aggregates, including **MAX** and **MIN**, share some other restrictions on their use. For one thing, aggregates cannot be nested, i.e., the value passed to an aggregate can't include some other aggregate. Also, aggregates cannot appear in a **WHERE** clause. To find the name of the teacher with the highest salary, for example, you *can't* just type

```
SELECT teacher_name
    FROM TEACHERS
    WHERE salary = MAX(salary);
```

This query is illegal. Instead, specifying conditions including aggregates requires using either **GROUP BY** and the **HAVING** clause, described at the end of this chapter, or, more likely, a subquery, described in Chapter 6.

Example: finding a maximum value

• *Problem*

What is the largest salary paid to a teacher?

• *Query Diagram*

TEACHERS
teacher# ⚷
teacher_name
phone
salary
✓   MAX(salary)

• *SQL*

```
SELECT MAX(salary)
   FROM TEACHERS;
```

• *Results*

MAX(salary)
_____

38200.00
_____

Example: finding a minimum value

• Problem

What is the lowest grade earned by a student?

• Query Diagram

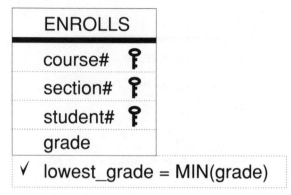

• SQL

```
SELECT lowest_grade = MIN(grade)
    FROM ENROLLS;
```

• Results

```
lowest_grade
```

_____

                     0

_____

Totalling Columns

Another useful piece of information to extract from a table is the total of all values in a particular column. The president of this university, for example, might wish to know the total of all teacher salaries. To allow this, SQL provides the **SUM** aggregate. As its name suggests, **SUM** returns the sum of a particular column. To answer his question, the president could type

```
SELECT SUM(salary)
    FROM TEACHERS;
```

The result would be a single value, the total of all teacher salaries.

It is also possible to determine the sum of a column's values only for records meeting some specific criteria. For example, to see the total salaries for all teachers earning over $30,000, the query is

```
SELECT SUM(salary)
    FROM TEACHERS
    WHERE salary > 30000;
```

Like **MAX** and **MIN**, **SUM** cannot be used exactly like an ordinary column name in a query. Because it returns only a single value, it may only be used by itself or with other aggregates that also return a single value, such as **MAX** and **MIN**. Also like **MAX** and **MIN**, **SUM** ignores any **NULL** values it encounters in the specified column.

Example: totalling a column's values

• Problem

What is the total of all teacher salaries?

• Query Diagram

TEACHERS	
teacher#	🔑
teacher_name	
phone	
salary	
✓ SUM(salary)	

• SQL

```
SELECT SUM(salary)
    FROM TEACHERS;
```

• Results

```
SUM(salary)
```

_____

190626.00

_____

Example: totalling only some of a column's values

• *Problem*

What is the total salary for all teachers earning over $30,000?

• *Query Diagram*

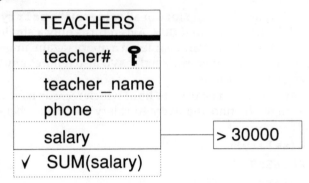

• *SQL*

```
SELECT SUM(salary)
    FROM TEACHERS
    WHERE salary > 30000;
```

• *Results*

```
SUM(salary)
```

```
    133526.00
```

Finding Averages

One more useful piece of information is the average of a column's values. To answer questions like this, SQL provides the **AVG** aggregate. To learn the average teacher's salary, for instance, one could type

```
SELECT AVG(salary)
   FROM TEACHERS;
```

The result of this query is the average of all values in the **salary** column of the **TEACHERS** table. Like **MAX**, **MIN**, and **SUM**, **AVG** returns only a single value, and so cannot be mixed with regular column names in a query (again, unless **GROUP BY** is used, as described later). And unsurprisingly, **AVG** also ignores any **NULL** values it encounters in the specified column.

Again, a **WHERE** clause can be used to limit which records have their values included in the average. To find the average salary for all teachers earning over $30,000, one could type

```
SELECT AVG(salary)
   FROM TEACHERS
   WHERE salary > 30000;
```

Example: averaging a column's values

• Problem

What is the average of all teacher salaries?

• Query Diagram

TEACHERS
teacher#   🔑
teacher_name
phone
salary
✓   AVG(salary)

• SQL

```
SELECT AVG(salary)
    FROM TEACHERS;
```

• Results

```
AVG(salary)
```

```
31771.00
```

Counting Records

Yet another facility SQL gives its users is the ability to count the number of records in a table which meet some specified criteria. This is accomplished with the **COUNT** aggregate. **COUNT** appears where the column names would normally go in a **SELECT** statement and is followed either by one or more column names or by just an asterisk. Both the column names and the asterisk must be enclosed in parentheses. To learn how many students are enrolled, one could type either

    SELECT COUNT(student_name)
        FROM STUDENTS;

or just

    SELECT COUNT(*)
        FROM STUDENTS;

Since **student_name** appears in every record in the table, both queries probably would produce the same results. If any of the values for **student_name** were **NULL**, however, the two queries almost certainly would *not* produce equivalent results. When counting, the **COUNT** function with a column name specified ignores **NULL** values, so any student names which were **NULL** would not be counted by the first query. With **COUNT(*)**, however, all records are counted, regardless of whether they contain **NULL**s. (One other note: according to the SQL standard, the first query shown above is illegal. The standard insists that whenever a column name is used instead of an asterisk, that column name must be preceded by the word **DISTINCT**, whose use is described in the next section. Many implementations of SQL do not enforce this requirement, however.)

As with other aggregates, the records to be counted can be restricted using a **WHERE** clause. Using our same example of well-paid teachers, we could learn how many of them earn over $30,000 by typing

    SELECT COUNT(*)
        FROM TEACHERS
        WHERE salary > 30000;

Like **MAX**, **MIN**, and **AVG**, **COUNT** returns a single value, and therefore can't be mixed with regular column names in a query (except with **GROUP BY**, described shortly). And unlike **AVG** and **SUM**, but like **MAX** and **MIN**, **COUNT** can be used on both character and numeric columns.

Example: counting values in a table

• *Problem*

How many students are there?

• *Query Diagram*

STUDENTS
student# 🔑
student_name
address
city
state
zip
sex
✓ COUNT(*)

• *SQL*

```
SELECT COUNT(*)
    FROM STUDENTS;
```

• *Results*

COUNT (*)

```
_____
         12
_____
```

Example: counting values in a table

• Problem

How many teachers earn over $30,000?

• Query Diagram

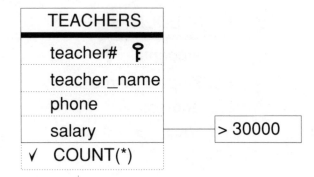

• SQL

```
SELECT COUNT(*)
   FROM TEACHERS
   WHERE salary > 30000;
```

• Results

COUNT(*)

_____

4

_____

Using DISTINCT

It's often the case that several records in a table will contain the same value in one or more of their fields. Sometimes, it can be useful to form queries which select each of those duplicate values only once. We may, for instance, wish to know from how many different states the students in this university come. For answering questions like this, SQL provides the **DISTINCT** option.

DISTINCT can be used in two somewhat different ways. When used with **COUNT** and the other aggregates, the word **DISTINCT** can appear before the column name, like

```
SELECT COUNT(DISTINCT state)
    FROM STUDENTS;
```

Adding **DISTINCT** before **state** tells SQL that each time the same value appears more than once in that column, only one of those values should be counted. This query, therefore, will return the number of *different* student home states. If desired, **DISTINCT** can also be used with **SUM**, **AVG**, and other parts of the language.

Using **DISTINCT** on a column where no two records have the same value is legal, but not very useful. One could, for instance, type

```
SELECT COUNT(DISTINCT student#)
    FROM STUDENTS;
```

but because no two values for **student#** are the same, the results would be just the same as those from

```
SELECT COUNT(student#)
    FROM STUDENTS;
```

(As mentioned earlier, the SQL standard requires **DISTINCT** before a column name used with the **COUNT** aggregate, but many implementations don't enforce this.)

DISTINCT can also be used on queries which do not use aggregates. In this case, the word **DISTINCT** appears immediately after the word **SELECT** but before the list of column names. Because we will often select the values from only a subset of the columns in a table, our results may contain duplicate records even though all complete records in the original table were unique. **DISTINCT** can be used to list only one occurrence of any duplicates which would otherwise appear.

Suppose, for instance, that we wished to list alphabetically the different states from which students come. We could do this with

```
SELECT state
    FROM STUDENTS
    ORDER BY state;
```

The results of this query, which doesn't use **DISTINCT**, are

```
state
_____

CA
CN
DE
IL
IL
MA
NY
PA
PA
PA
RI
VA
_____
```

If the **DISTINCT** option is used, however, like

    SELECT DISTINCT state

       FROM STUDENTS

       ORDER BY state;

duplicates are eliminated from the results, yielding

```
state
_____

CA
CN
DE
IL
MA
NY
PA
RI
VA
_____
```

Example: using DISTINCT *to count unique values*

• Problem

How many different states do students come from?

• Query Diagram

STUDENTS
student#   🔑
student_name
address
city
state
zip
sex
✓ COUNT(DISTINCT state)

• SQL

```
SELECT COUNT(DISTINCT state)
    FROM STUDENTS;
```

• Results

COUNT(DISTINCT state)

9

Grouping Selected Data

With all the flexibility described so far for retrieving data from a table, one major function has not yet been discussed: using **GROUP BY** to organize the selected data into groups. When used with aggregates, **GROUP BY** controls the level at which the aggregates are computed. For example, with **GROUP BY** we could find the maximum grade in each section of each course, or the average number of students taught by each teacher.

The general form of a **SELECT** statement using **GROUP BY** is

```
SELECT <column names>
    FROM <table>
    <WHERE clause>
    GROUP BY <column names>
    ORDER BY <column names>;
```

As always, the first **<column names>** and **<table>** indicate the columns which should be selected from the named table. A **<WHERE clause>** may optionally appear, specifying restrictions which individual records must meet to be selected. Next appears **GROUP BY** and its **<column names>**, indicating which column or columns contain the values to be used in forming the groups. Optionally, the **SELECT** statement may end with an **ORDER BY** followed by one or more **<column names>** by whose values the results should be ordered. The column names following both **GROUP BY** and **ORDER BY** must be drawn from those specified immediately after **SELECT**.

Consider, for example, the information contained in the **ENROLLS** table. For each class in which a student is currently enrolled, this table contains a record indicating that student's **student#**, the class's **course#** and **section#**, and the **grade** that student has received. Several students have more than one record in this table, since they are enrolled in more than one class.

Suppose we wish to know the number of students in each course. One way to learn this would be to simply list the entire table, ordered by course number, then actually count the number of records for each course. Using **GROUP BY** and the **COUNT** aggregate, however, we can let SQL do the counting for us. For example, the query

```
SELECT course#, num_enrolled = COUNT(*)
    FROM ENROLLS
    GROUP BY course#;
```

would return two columns of information: the first a list of course numbers, the second, entitled **num_enrolled**, a count of the number of students enrolled in that course. This query is (conceptually) processed as follows: first, the chosen fields from each record in **ENROLLS** are placed in ascending order according to **course#**. If it were printed, the table would now look like this:

course#	section#	student#	grade
290	1	548	2
290	1	298	3
290	1	349	4
450	2	210	3
450	1	473	2
450	1	654	4
450	2	548	
480	1	410	2
480	2	473	0
480	1	649	4
480	2	298	3
480	1	358	4
730	1	348	2
730	1	148	3
730	1	473	3
730	1	210	1
730	1	649	4
730	1	558	3

Next, the **COUNT(*)** operation is applied to each group of records which contain the same value for **course#**. All the records with a **course#** value of 290 make up the first group, while all those with a **course#** of 450 make up the second group, and so on. Finally, the results of the query are displayed, with each course number listed only once, followed by a count of the number of students in each course. Those results are

course#	num_enrolled
290	3
450	4
480	5
730	6

Recall that earlier we said that aggregates like **COUNT** always returned only a single value, and so could only be used in limited ways. When using **GROUP BY**, such operations return a single value for each *group*, and so can be pressed into service in a more versatile way. **GROUP BY** places restrictions on exactly how we can use column names in a query, however. In particular, the column names following **SELECT** must either be part of aggregates, such as **COUNT** or **AVG**, or they must appear as one of the column names in the **GROUP BY** clause.

For instance, suppose we wished to learn both the number of courses in which a student was enrolled and his or her average grade. A query which accomplishes this is

```
SELECT student#, AVG(grade), courses = COUNT(*)
    FROM ENROLLS
    GROUP BY student#;
```

As before, the **ENROLLS** table is first ordered (again, conceptually) by **student#**. Next, the two operations specified, **AVG** and **COUNT**, are applied to each group of records with the same value for **student#**. Finally, the results are displayed in three columns, labelled **student#**, **AVG(grade)**, and **courses**.

Example: grouping selected data with GROUP BY

• Problem

List the number of students enrolled in each course.

• Query Diagram

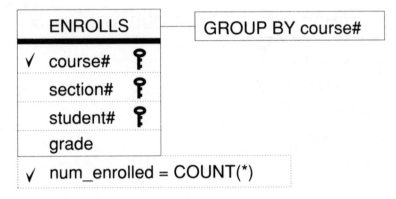

• SQL

```
SELECT course#, num_enrolled = COUNT(*)
    FROM ENROLLS
    GROUP BY course#;
```

• Results

```
course# num_enrolled
```

course#	num_enrolled
290	3
450	4
480	5
730	6

Example: grouping selected data with GROUP BY

• Problem

List the number of courses taken by each student.

• Query Diagram

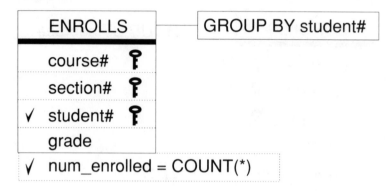

• SQL

```
SELECT student#, num_enrolled = COUNT(*)
    FROM ENROLLS
    GROUP BY student#;
```

• Results

student#	num_enrolled
148	1
210	2
298	2
348	1
349	1
358	1
410	1
473	3
548	1
558	1
649	2
654	1

Example: grouping selected data with GROUP BY

• Problem

List the average grade and number of courses taken by each student.

• Query Diagram

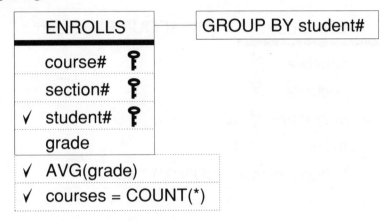

• SQL

```
SELECT student#, AVG(grade), courses = COUNT(*)
    FROM ENROLLS
    GROUP BY student#;
```

• Results

student#	AVG(grade)	courses
148	3.00	1
210	2.00	2
298	3.00	2
348	2.00	1
349	4.00	1
358	4.00	1
410	2.00	1
473	1.67	3
548	2.00	1
558	3.00	1
649	4.00	2
654	4.00	1

Example: grouping selected data with GROUP BY

• Problem

Assuming a fee of $450.00 per course, determine each student's total tuition bill.

• Query Diagram

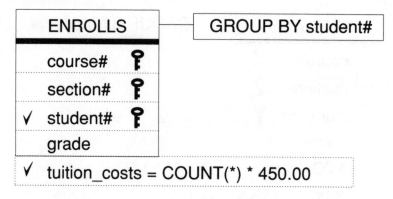

• SQL

```
SELECT student#, tuition_costs = COUNT(*) * 450.00
  FROM ENROLLS
  GROUP BY student#;
```

• Results

student#	tuition_costs
148	450.00
210	900.00
298	900.00
348	450.00
349	450.00
358	450.00
410	450.00
473	1350.00
548	450.00
558	450.00
649	900.00
654	450.00

Example: grouping selected data with GROUP BY

• Problem

List the average grade and number of students for each section of each course.

• Query Diagram

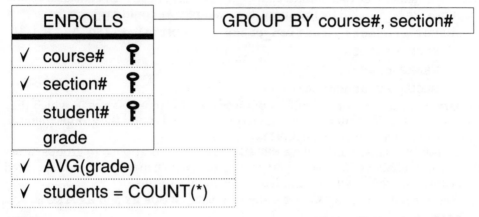

ENROLLS	GROUP BY course#, section#
✓ course#	
✓ section#	
student#	
grade	
✓ AVG(grade)	
✓ students = COUNT(*)	

• SQL

```
SELECT course#, section#, AVG(grade),
       students = COUNT(*)
   FROM ENROLLS
   GROUP BY course#, section#;
```

• Results

course#	section#	AVG(grade)	students
290	1	3.00	3
450	1	3.00	2
450	2	3.00	2
480	1	3.33	3
480	2	1.50	2
730	1	2.67	6

More on Grouping: the HAVING Clause

Using **GROUP BY** is in some ways like doing several queries simultaneously on a single table. As with most queries, though, we would like some way to restrict the values of records which are included in the query. Up to now, this has always been done with a **WHERE** clause. Using **WHERE** clauses with **GROUP BY** can be tricky, however. Remember that **WHERE** clauses specify criteria which *individual records* must meet to be selected by the query. For example, we could say

```
SELECT student#, tuition_costs = COUNT(*) * 450.00
    FROM ENROLLS
    WHERE grade = 2.0
    GROUP BY student#;
```

to learn what each student's tuition bill was only for those classes in which they received a C (2.0) or better. If we want to place restrictions on the groups themselves, however, we must use the **HAVING** clause.

A **HAVING** clause works like a **WHERE** clause, but it is applied to groups rather than to individual records. Now, only those *groups* which meet the criteria specified in the **HAVING** clause will be included in the query's results.

The general form of a **SELECT** statement using **GROUP BY** and **HAVING** is

```
SELECT <column names>
    FROM <table>
    <WHERE clause>
    GROUP BY <column names>
    HAVING <predicate>
    ORDER BY <column names>;
```

As before, the first occurrence of **<column names>** and **<table>** indicate the columns which should be selected from the named table. The **<WHERE clause>** may optionally appear (placing restrictions only on values of individual records selected for the groups), followed by **GROUP BY** and one or more **<column names>**, indicating the column or columns to be used in forming the groups. Next comes the word **HAVING** and a **<predicate>**, specifying the conditions which the groups themselves must meet. And once again, the **SELECT** may optionally end with an **ORDER BY** followed by one or more **<column names>**.

For example, to see the average grade and number of courses taken only by those students with an average grade greater than 2.5, one could type

```
SELECT student#, AVG(grade), courses = COUNT(*)
    FROM ENROLLS
    GROUP BY student#
    HAVING AVG(grade) > 2.50;
```

A **WHERE** clause could not be used in this case, since the restriction on average grades of students applies only to each group, not to each record.

Similarly, to see the average grade and number of students for only those sections with more than four students, the query would be

```
SELECT section#, AVG(grade), students = COUNT(*)
    FROM ENROLLS
    GROUP BY section#
    HAVING COUNT(*) > 4;
```

Again, a **WHERE** clause could not be used, since the restriction of having more than four students applies to each group, not to any of the individual records within a group. In both this and the previous example, the groups appearing in the results of each query are restricted to those which meet the requirements specified in the **HAVING** clause.

A **HAVING** clause may also be used without **GROUP BY**. In this case, it places a restriction on the *entire* result of the query. With no **GROUP BY** clause specified, those results are treated as one big group.

Using **HAVING** without **GROUP BY** might seem useless, and in most cases it is. When used with certain kinds of subqueries, however, as described in Chapter 6, **HAVING** clauses can be quite useful on their own.

Example: specifying a property for grouped data with HAVING

• *Problem*

List the average grade and number of courses taken by students with an average grade of more than 2.5.

• *Query Diagram*

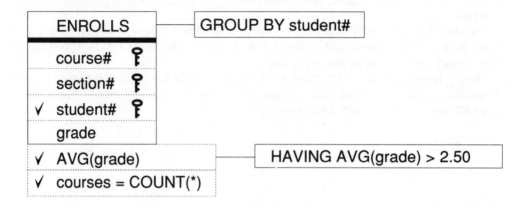

• *SQL*

```
SELECT student#, AVG(grade), courses = COUNT(*)
    FROM ENROLLS
    GROUP BY student#
    HAVING AVG(grade) > 2.50;
```

• *Results*

student#	AVG(grade)	courses
148	3.00	1
298	3.00	2
349	4.00	1
358	4.00	1
558	3.00	1
649	4.00	2
654	4.00	1

Example: specifying a property for grouped data with HAVING

• *Problem*

List the average grade and number of students for each section with more than four students.

• *Query Diagram*

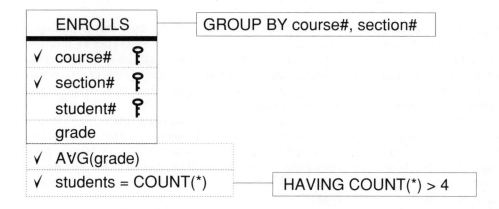

• *SQL*

```
SELECT course#, section#, AVG(grade),
     students = COUNT(*)
  FROM ENROLLS
  GROUP BY course#, section#
  HAVING COUNT(*) > 4;
```

• *Results*

course#	section#	AVG(grade)	students
730	1	2.67	6

Retrieving Data From Several Tables: Joins

5

Every query we have seen so far retrieves data from only a single table. If all of a database's information were contained in one large table, these types of queries would be all that was required. Practically, though, storing all the information in just one table would require maintaining several duplicate copies of the same values. In real systems, therefore, all but the very simplest databases divide their information among several different tables.

Both in real databases and in our simple example database, then, many interesting questions cannot be answered by retrieving data from only a single table. Instead, we must form queries which simultaneously access two or more tables. Any query that extracts data from more than one table must perform a *join*. As its name suggests, a join means that some or all of the specified tables' contents are joined together in the results of the query.

Qualified Names

In every **SELECT** statement, we must indicate the names of the columns we are interested in. So far, all of those columns have been from the same table. With joins, however, we will be selecting columns from two or more tables simultaneously. Although all of the columns in a single table must have unique names, columns in two different tables may have the same name. To identify a column in the database uniquely, then, we must use its *qualified name*.

A qualified name consists of the name of a table, followed by a period and the name of a column in that table. For example, the qualified name for the **teacher#** column in the **SECTIONS** table is **SECTIONS.teacher#**, while the qualified name for that same column in the **TEACHERS** table is **TEACHERS.teacher#**. Because every column in a table must have a different name, and because SQL requires every table in a database to have a different name, a qualified name is guaranteed to identify exactly one column in exactly one table.

To see how qualified names are used in a query, suppose that we wished to see each value for **teacher_name** from **TEACHERS** along with each possible value for **teacher#** and **course#** from **SECTIONS**. Requesting **teacher_name** from **TEACHERS** along with **course#** from **SECTIONS** is easy: both column names are unique in the database. But selecting **teacher#** from **SECTIONS** requires using the qualified name for **teacher#**, since a column with that name appears in both tables. A formulation of this query might be

```
SELECT teacher_name, SECTIONS.teacher#, course#
    FROM TEACHERS, SECTIONS;
```

(What are the results of this query? Probably not what you'd expect—see the next section.)

As we have already seen, qualified names are not required when there is no possibility of ambiguity. In the above query, for instance, just the column name was required for **course#**, since **TEACHERS** and **SECTIONS** have only one column with this name between them. Despite the fact that a column called **course#** also appears in the **COURSES** table, the list of tables in the above query's **FROM** clause limits its scope to **TEACHERS** and **SECTIONS**.

We have been taking advantage of this automatic limitation all along. For instance, in the query

```
SELECT student#
    FROM STUDENTS;
```

student# must refer to the column of that name in the **STUDENTS** table. Similarly, in the query

```
SELECT teacher#
    FROM TEACHERS;
```

there is still no ambiguity, because the **FROM** clause specifies from which table the values for **teacher#** are to be drawn. Even simple queries can use qualified names if desired, like

```
SELECT STUDENTS.student_name
    FROM STUDENTS;
```

although it's hard to see why this would be useful. In the first example given above, however, ambiguity was possible, and so a qualified name was required. Because it is always legal to use qualified names, even when they're not required, another way to express that first query would have been

```
SELECT TEACHERS.teacher_name, SECTIONS.teacher#,
       SECTIONS.course#
    FROM TEACHERS, SECTIONS;
```

What is a Join?

What are the results of the first query above? If you type

```
SELECT teacher_name, SECTIONS.teacher#, course#
    FROM TEACHERS, SECTIONS;
```

what will come back in return? Obviously, the result will have three columns: **teacher_name**, **SECTIONS.teacher#**, and **course#**. But what values will be contained in those three columns?

To carry out this query, SQL will list values from each record of both tables. In fact, it will list all possible combinations of the selected columns from all records in the two tables. In other words, the results will begin with a line containing the values of **teacher#** and **course#** from the first record in **SECTIONS** matched with the value of **teacher_name** from the first record in **TEACHERS**. Next will come a line matching the next **teacher_name** with the selected values from the first record in the **SECTIONS** table, and so on, until each of the records in the **TEACHERS** table has been matched with the first **SECTIONS** record. Next, the results will contain a series of lines that match the selected values from the second record in **SECTIONS** with the **teacher_name** value from every record in the **TEACHERS** table, and so on. The result of this seemingly simple query is a long list of combinations, each consisting of a value from a record in **TEACHERS** paired with two values from a record in **SEC-TIONS**.

Example: a simple join

• *Problem*

List all teacher names along with all the values for teacher number and course number contained in the **SECTIONS** table.

• *Query Diagram*

TEACHERS	
teacher#	♀
✓ teacher_name	
phone	
salary	

SECTIONS	
✓ course#	♀
section#	♀
✓ teacher#	
num_students	

• *SQL*

```
SELECT teacher_name, SECTIONS.teacher#, course#
    FROM TEACHERS, SECTIONS;
```

• Results

teacher_name	SECTIONS.teacher#	course#
Dr. Horn	303	450
Dr. Lowe	303	450
Dr. Engle	303	450
Dr. Cooke	303	450
Dr. Olsen	303	450
Dr. Scango	303	450
Dr. Horn	290	730
Dr. Lowe	290	730
Dr. Engle	290	730
Dr. Cooke	290	730
Dr. Olsen	290	730
Dr. Scango	290	730
Dr. Horn	430	290
Dr. Lowe	430	290
Dr. Engle	430	290
Dr. Cooke	430	290
Dr. Olsen	430	290
Dr. Scango	430	290
Dr. Horn	180	480
Dr. Lowe	180	480
Dr. Engle	180	480
Dr. Cooke	180	480
Dr. Olsen	180	480
Dr. Scango	180	480
Dr. Horn	560	450
Dr. Lowe	560	450
Dr. Engle	560	450
Dr. Cooke	560	450
Dr. Olsen	560	450
Dr. Scango	560	450
Dr. Horn	784	480
Dr. Lowe	784	480
Dr. Engle	784	480
Dr. Cooke	784	480
Dr. Olsen	784	480
Dr. Scango	784	480

Restricting the Results of a Join

What happens if, in a query accessing two tables with columns of the same name, we specify the same column name twice, once for each table? Doing this requires that we give the qualified name for each, like

```
SELECT teacher_name, TEACHERS.teacher#,
        SECTIONS.teacher#, course#
FROM TEACHERS, SECTIONS;
```

The results are like those specified above—a list of all possible combinations of the selected columns from the two tables—except that the column called **teacher#** appears twice. The results of this query are:

teacher_name	TEACHERS.teacher#	SECTIONS.teacher#	course#
Dr. Horn	303	303	450
Dr. Lowe	290	303	450
Dr. Engle	30	303	450
Dr. Cooke	180	303	450
Dr. Olsen	560	303	450
Dr. Scango	784	303	450
Dr. Horn	303	290	730
Dr. Lowe	290	290	730
Dr. Engle	430	290	730
Dr. Cooke	180	290	730
Dr. Olsen	560	290	730
Dr. Scango	784	290	730
Dr. Horn	303	430	290
Dr. Lowe	290	430	290
Dr. Engle	430	430	290
Dr. Cooke	180	430	290
Dr. Olsen	560	430	290
Dr. Scango	784	430	290
Dr. Horn	303	180	480
Dr. Lowe	290	180	480
Dr. Engle	430	180	480
Dr. Cooke	180	180	480
Dr. Olsen	560	180	480
Dr. Scango	784	180	480
Dr. Horn	303	560	450
Dr. Lowe	290	560	450
Dr. Engle	430	560	450
Dr. Cooke	180	560	450
Dr. Olsen	560	560	450
Dr. Scango	784	560	450

Dr. Horn	303	784	480
Dr. Lowe	290	784	480
Dr. Engle	430	784	480
Dr. Cooke	180	784	480
Dr. Olsen	560	784	480
Dr. Scango	784	784	480

As always, each column is labelled with the appropriate name, so for the two **teacher#** columns, both column names are qualified names. These two columns contain all possible combinations of values for **teacher#** from the two tables.

Usually, such general results as these are not very useful. Too much information is given, and it is difficult to pick out what's interesting. To reduce the size of the results and thereby zero in on the answer to some particular question, we can add a **WHERE** clause to the above query. We might wish to know, for example, which teachers are teaching which courses. Further, we may wish to identify those teachers by name, not just by their teacher numbers. This information is available in the results from the query above, but it is not in a very concise or usable form. By adding a **WHERE** clause, we can retrieve only those results of the join in which we are interested.

To see which teachers teach which courses, look through the results just given. Note that whenever the value of **teacher#** from the **TEACHERS** table is equal to the value of **teacher#** from the **SECTIONS** table, the course whose **course#** appears in that record is one which is taught by that teacher. Because of the way this database is defined, the two **teacher#** columns must have this relationship. Columns like these, sometimes called *join columns*, exist in each of the tables in our example database. Similar columns will also exist in most or all of the tables in real relational databases. The information stored in these join columns gives us a very powerful tool for accessing the stored data.

Back to the original question: which teachers teach which classes? To select just those records from the mass of information given above, one could type

```
SELECT teacher_name, SECTIONS.teacher#, course#
    FROM TEACHERS, SECTIONS
    WHERE TEACHERS.teacher# = SECTIONS.teacher#;
```

The results are only those records which meet the condition specified in the **WHERE** clause: those where the two **teacher#** values are equal. We can now see easily which courses are taught by each teacher, with teachers identified by name:

teacher_name	SECTIONS.teacher#	course#
Dr. Horn	303	450
Dr. Lowe	290	730
Dr. Engle	430	290
Dr. Cooke	180	480
Dr. Olsen	560	450
Dr. Scango	784	480

Even though they are used in the **WHERE** clause, the values for **teacher#** need not be selected by the query. If we were interested in seeing only teachers' names and the numbers of the courses they teach, we would have typed

```
SELECT teacher_name, course#
    FROM TEACHERS, SECTIONS
    WHERE TEACHERS.teacher# = SECTIONS.teacher#;
```

This time, the results include only the **teacher_name** and **course#** values for those records which meet the **WHERE** clause's condition, i.e., a list of teachers and the courses taught by each.

Because the **SECTIONS** table contains records only for currently offered sections, we could see only the names of those teachers who are currently teaching some section with

```
SELECT teacher_name
    FROM TEACHERS, SECTIONS
    WHERE TEACHERS.teacher# = SECTIONS.teacher#;
```

Since all teachers in our sample database are assigned to a section, the **teacher_name**s listed by this query are identical to those of the previous one. The important thing about this example, though, is its **FROM** clause: despite the fact that no values from the **SECTIONS** table are selected, that table must still appear in the **FROM** clause, since a value from **SECTIONS** *is* referenced in the **WHERE** clause. The names of all tables which have any of their columns referenced anywhere in the query must appear in the query's **FROM** clause.

Query Diagrams for Joins

With joins using **WHERE** clauses, the visual approach to SQL really comes into its own. The columns from the tables being joined, such as **TEACHERS.teacher#** and **SECTIONS.teacher#** above, are indicated by a line connecting them. This line is marked with the operator used in the **WHERE** clause, typically an equal sign. For more complex joins involving more than two tables, several such connecting lines will exist between tables.

Joins can get complicated. By first thinking of (or actually drawing) the query visually, this complexity becomes manageable.

Example: a join with a simple WHERE clause

• Problem

Which teachers teach which courses? (List the teachers by name.)

• Query Diagram

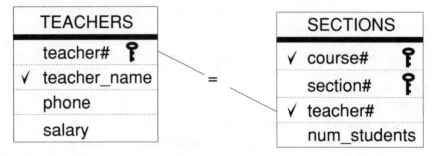

• SQL

```
SELECT teacher_name, SECTIONS.teacher#, course#
    FROM TEACHERS, SECTIONS
    WHERE TEACHERS.teacher# = SECTIONS.teacher#;
```

• Results

teacher_name	SECTIONS.teacher#	course#
Dr. Horn	303	450
Dr. Lowe	290	730
Dr. Engle	430	290
Dr. Cooke	180	480
Dr. Olsen	560	450
Dr. Scango	784	480

• Note

If we were willing to settle for identifying teachers solely by their **teacher#**, no join would be required. The **SECTIONS** table alone contains enough information to answer that question. By requesting the *names* of teachers, however, we also request a join, since teacher names and teacher numbers are not stored in the same table.

Example: a join with a simple WHERE clause

• Problem

What is the enrollment in each section of each course?

• Query Diagram

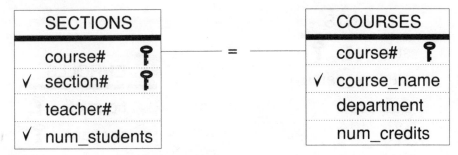

• SQL

```
SELECT section#, course_name, num_students
    FROM SECTIONS, COURSES
    WHERE SECTIONS.course# = COURSES.course#;
```

• Results

section#	course_name	num_students
1	Western Civilization	2
2	Western Civilization	2
1	Calculus IV	6
1	English Composition	3
1	Compiler Writing	3
2	Compiler Writing	2

Example: a join with a simple WHERE *clause*

• Problem

List the grades received by each student.

• Query Diagram

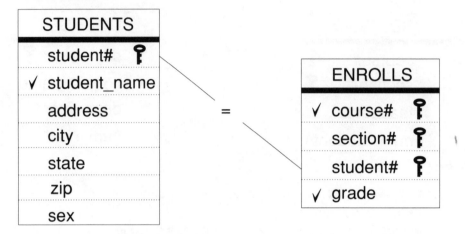

•SQL

```
SELECT student_name, course#, grade
    FROM STUDENTS, ENROLLS
    WHERE STUDENTS.student# = ENROLLS.student#;
```

• Results

student_name	course#	grade
Susan Powell	730	3
Bob Dawson	450	3
Bob Dawson	730	1
Howard Mansfield	290	3
Howard Mansfield	480	3
Susan Pugh	730	2
Joe Adams	290	4
Bill Jones	480	2
Carol Dean	450	2
Carol Dean	730	3
Carol Dean	480	0
Allen Thomas	290	2
Allen Thomas	450	
Val Shipp	730	3
John Anderson	730	4
John Anderson	480	4
Janet Thomas	450	4

Manipulating the Results of a Join

Just as with queries which access a single table, queries accessing two or more tables can use the full power of SQL. For instance, all options of the **WHERE** clause are available, including **LIKE** and **NOT LIKE**, **IN** and **NOT IN**, **NULL** and **NOT NULL**, and **AND**, **OR**, and **NOT**. Also, arithmetic operations can be performed on the results before they are displayed, just as with simpler queries. And by using **ORDER BY**, the results of a join can be listed in either ascending or descending order, based on the values of any selected column.

The aggregates described in the previous chapter can also be applied. To learn the number of rows in a table, for example, the **COUNT** aggregate can be used, while average values can be computed with **AVG**. In general, SQL's features are additive: its basic tools can also be used in more complex contexts, such as within joins.

Example: using a more complicated WHERE *clause in a join*

• Problem

Which students from California or Illinois got A's or B's?

• Query Diagram

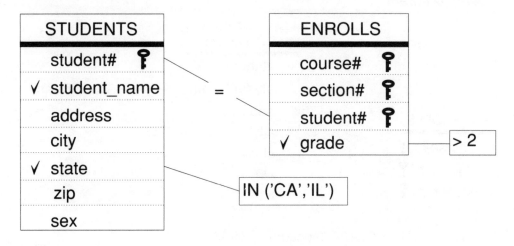

• SQL

```
SELECT student_name, state, grade
    FROM STUDENTS, ENROLLS
    WHERE state IN ('CA','IL') AND
        grade > 2 AND
        STUDENTS.student# = ENROLLS.student#;
```

• Results

student_name	state	grade
Val Shipp	IL	3

Example: performing arithmetic operations with a join

• *Problem*

Assuming that tuition is $450.00 per course, what is Carol Dean's total tuition bill?

• *Query Diagram*

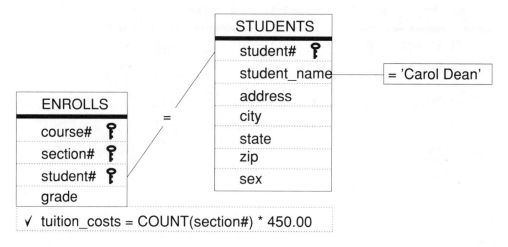

√ tuition_costs = COUNT(section#) * 450.00

• *SQL*

```
SELECT tuition_costs = COUNT(section#) * 450.00
    FROM ENROLLS, STUDENTS
    WHERE student_name = 'Carol Dean' AND
          ENROLLS.student# = STUDENTS.student#;
```

• *Results*

```
tuition_costs
```

```
1350.00
```

Example: ordering the results of a join with ORDER BY

• Problem

List the teacher for and number of students in each section. Order this list of courses by number of students, from largest to smallest.

• Query Diagram

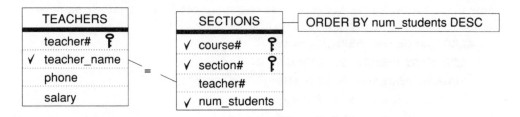

• SQL

```
SELECT teacher_name, course#, section#, num_students
    FROM TEACHERS, SECTIONS
    WHERE TEACHERS.teacher# = SECTIONS.teacher#
    ORDER BY num_students DESC;
```

• Results

teacher_name	course#	section#	num_students
Dr. Lowe	730	1	6
Dr. Cooke	480	1	3
Dr. Engle	290	1	3
Dr. Horn	450	1	2
Dr. Olsen	450	2	2
Dr. Scango	480	2	2

Aliases

Every table in a database must have a unique name. Sometimes it is useful to assign an *alias* to a table, a name which can be used in place of the table's real name. Aliases, called "correlation names" in the SQL standard, exist only for the life of a particular query, e.g., for the duration of one **SELECT** statement. A common reason to use aliases is to reduce the amount of typing required to enter a query.

To create an alias name for a table, simply type the alias name after the table name in the **FROM** clause. Leave at least one space between the table's name and the alias. For example, the query

```
SELECT student_name, grade
    FROM STUDENTS S, ENROLLS E
    WHERE course# = 450 AND
          section# = 1 AND
          S.student# = E.student#;
```

defines two aliases: **S** for **STUDENTS**, and **E** for **ENROLLS**. This query could also be entered as

```
SELECT student_name, grade
    FROM STUDENTS, ENROLLS
    WHERE course# = 450 AND
          section# = 1 AND
          STUDENTS.student# = ENROLLS.student#;
```

and the results would be identical. The only difference is in the number of characters typed.

If qualified names are used in specifying the selected columns, it is even possible to use an alias before it is defined. We could, for example, say

```
SELECT C.department, C.course#, S.section#,
       S.num_students
    FROM COURSES C, SECTIONS S
    WHERE S.course# = C.course#;
```

Here, the aliases are defined as always in the **FROM** clause, but are used in both the qualified names and the **WHERE** clause.

Because their most common use is to reduce the amount of typing, alias names are often kept to a single character. It is legal, however, to use longer alias names. It's even possible to create an alias name which is longer than the original table name.

Example: using aliases in a join

• Problem

List the names and grades of all students enrolled in section 1 of course 450.

• Query Diagram

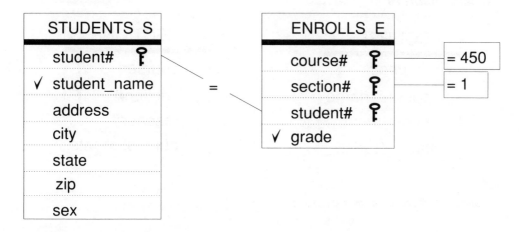

• SQL

```
SELECT student_name, grade
    FROM STUDENTS S, ENROLLS E
    WHERE course# = 450 AND
          section# = 1 AND
          S.student# = E.student#;
```

• Results

student_name	grade
Carol Dean	2
Janet Thomas	4

Example: using aliases in a join

• Problem

For each department, list its courses and sections together with the number of students in each.

• Query Diagram

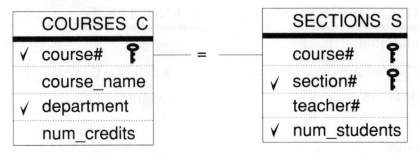

• SQL

```
SELECT C.department, C.course#,
       S.section#, S.num_students
   FROM COURSES C, SECTIONS S
   WHERE S.course# = C.course#;
```

• Results

C.department	C.course#	S.section#	S.num_students
History	450	1	2
History	450	2	2
Math	730	1	6
English	290	1	3
Computer Science	480	1	3
Computer Science	480	2	2

Joins With Three Tables

Earlier in this chapter, we saw which teachers taught which courses. In that example, the teachers were listed by both name and number, while the courses were listed by number only. We may also wish to list the courses by name. To do this, we must extract information from three different tables: **TEACHERS**, **SECTIONS**, and **COURSES**.

A join with three tables is a fairly straightforward extension of the two-table join. We must list all necessary tables in the **FROM** clause, then include appropriate restrictions in the **WHERE** clause. To answer the question posed above, we could type

```
SELECT teacher_name, SECTIONS.teacher#,
       SECTIONS.course#, course_name
   FROM TEACHERS, SECTIONS, COURSES
   WHERE TEACHERS.teacher# = SECTIONS.teacher# AND
         SECTIONS.course# = COURSES.course#;
```

The results contain the four named columns, each with values only for those records that meet the restrictions in the **WHERE** clause. In other words, this query produces a list of teachers and teacher numbers, together with both the names and numbers of the courses they teach.

(If you're still having trouble believing that the simple restrictions given in the **WHERE** clause produce the desired results, try the query without the **WHERE** clause. If you manually search through the results, you'll find that the resulting rows for which the conditions in the **WHERE** clause are true are exactly those desired.)

The Visual Approach With More Than Two Tables

Deciding exactly which columns from which tables should be joined can sometimes be difficult. With the visual approach, however, the task is greatly simplified. By referring to a diagram containing all of a database's tables, it is easy to see which tables contain which columns. With the aid of this diagram, one can "navigate" through the database, determining which columns should be joined to produce the desired information. Producing the correct SQL for the query becomes almost trivial once the visual picture of the query is understood.

Figure 5.1 shows every table in our example database. For each, a line has been drawn between the most likely "joinable" columns. By joining the various tables through the values contained in these columns, a wide range of queries can be expressed.

In this example, we have indicated which columns may be used for joins. In other databases, how can you learn which columns can be used for joins? The first hint is to look at the column names: often, joinable columns in different tables are given the same name, as we have done in the example database. To get at a more precise answer, though, notice that the connected columns in every table each contain the same *kinds* of values. The **section#** column in the **SECTIONS** table contains the same kinds of values as the **section#** column in the **ENROLLS** table: section numbers of various courses. Similarly, the **course#** columns in both the **SECTIONS** and **COURSES** tables contain the numbers of the courses themselves. In general, it makes sense to join two columns whenever they contain the same kinds

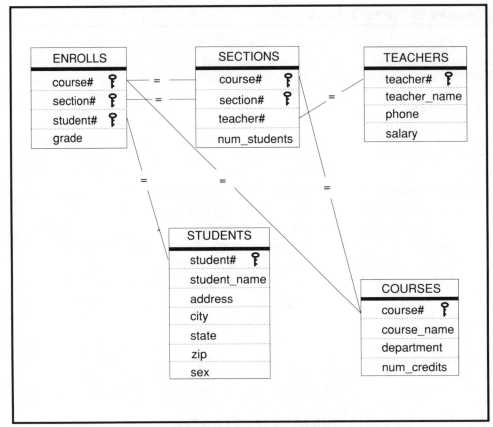

Figure 5.1 *Possible joins*

of values, such as course numbers. This is true regardless of the names assigned to those columns. If the column in the **SECTIONS** table containing course numbers were called **course_number**, it would still be legal to join it with the **course#** table in **COURSES**. As long as the two columns contain the same kinds of values, the join is possible.

Note also that each of the join columns indicated in Figure 5.1 is a key or part of a key. When key values from one table are stored in a column in another table, that column is said to contain a *foreign key*. A table's own key is sometimes referred to as its *primary key* to distinguish it from any foreign keys that table may contain. In Figure 5.1, for example, **teacher#** is the primary key for the **TEACHERS** table but is a foreign key in the **SECTIONS** table. Joins usually occur between columns containing either foreign or primary keys.

Example: joins with three tables

• Problem

List the names of all teachers, along with the names and numbers of the courses taught by each.

• Query Diagram

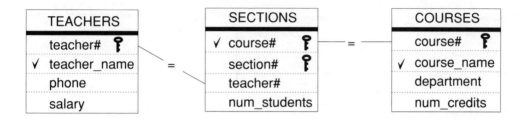

• SQL

```
SELECT teacher_name, SECTIONS.course#,
       course_name
  FROM TEACHERS, SECTIONS, COURSES
  WHERE TEACHERS.teacher# = SECTIONS.teacher# AND
        SECTIONS.course# = COURSES.course#;
```

• Results

teacher_name	SECTIONS.course#	course_name
Dr. Horn	450	Western Civilization
Dr. Olsen	450	Western Civilization
Dr. Lowe	730	Calculus IV
Dr. Engle	290	English Composition
Dr. Cooke	480	Compiler Writing
Dr. Scango	480	Compiler Writing

Example: joins with three tables

• *Problem*

In which courses did any female student get an A? (List both the courses and the students by name.)

• *Query Diagram*

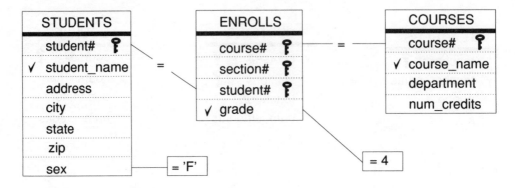

• *SQL*

```
SELECT student_name, course_name, grade
   FROM STUDENTS, ENROLLS, COURSES
   WHERE sex = 'F' AND
         grade = 4 AND
         STUDENTS.student# = ENROLLS.student# AND
         ENROLLS.course# = COURSES.course#;
```

• *Results*

student_name	course_name	grade
Janet Thomas	Western Civilization	4

Example: joins with three tables

• Problem

List the names of all teachers and their departments, ordered alphabetically by department.

• Query Diagram

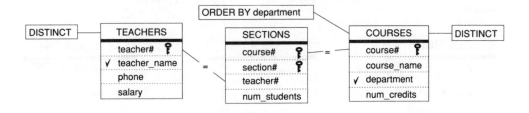

• SQL

```
SELECT DISTINCT teacher_name, department
    FROM TEACHERS, SECTIONS, COURSES
    WHERE TEACHERS.teacher# = SECTIONS.teacher# AND
          SECTIONS.course# = COURSES.course#
    ORDER BY department;
```

• Results

teacher_name	department
Dr. Cooke	Computer Science
Dr. Scango	Computer Science
Dr. Engle	English
Dr. Horn	History
Dr. Olsen	History
Dr. Lowe	Math

Example: joins with three tables

• *Problem*

List each student's grade for each course. Order the list alphabetically by course name, then, for each course, by student name.

• *Query Diagram*

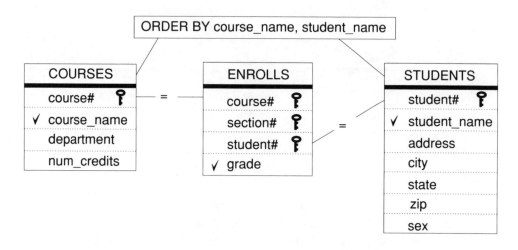

•*SQL*

```
SELECT course_name, student_name, grade
   FROM COURSES, ENROLLS, STUDENTS
   WHERE STUDENTS.student# = ENROLLS.student# AND
         ENROLLS.course# = COURSES.course#
   ORDER BY course_name, student_name;
```

• Results

course_name	student_name	grade
Calculus IV	Bob Dawson	1
Calculus IV	Carol Dean	3
Calculus IV	John Anderson	4
Calculus IV	Susan Powell	3
Calculus IV	Susan Pugh	2
Calculus IV	Val Shipp	3
Compiler Writing	Bill Jones	2
Compiler Writing	Carol Dean	0
Compiler Writing	Howard Mansfield	3
Compiler Writing	John Anderson	4
English Composition	Allen Thomas	2
English Composition	Howard Mansfield	3
English Composition	Joe Adams	4
Western Civilization	Allen Thomas	
Western Civilization	Bob Dawson	3
Western Civilization	Carol Dean	2
Western Civilization	Janet Thomas	4

• Note

Allen Thomas has yet to receive his grade in Western Civilization. Because this field in the corresponding record in the **ENROLLS** table contains a **NULL** value, no grade for that course appears in the result of this query.

Example: joins with three tables

• Problem

Which courses are the students from Pennsylvania, California, and Connecticut taking?

• Query Diagram

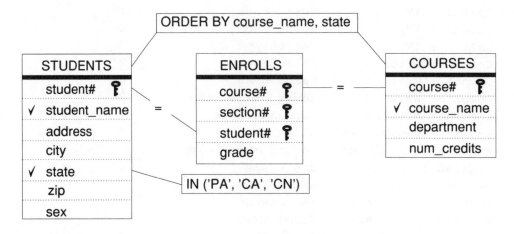

• SQL

```
SELECT student_name, course_name, state
    FROM STUDENTS, ENROLLS, COURSES
    WHERE state IN ('PA', 'CA', 'CN') AND
          STUDENTS.student# = ENROLLS.student# AND
          ENROLLS.course# = COURSES.course#
    ORDER BY course_name, state;
```

• Results

student_name	course_name	state
Susan Pugh	Calculus IV	CN
Susan Powell	Calculus IV	PA
Bill Jones	Compiler Writing	CA
Janet Thomas	Western Civilization	PA

Example: joins with three tables

• Problem

List alphabetically the names and grades of all male students enrolled in Calculus IV.

• Query Diagram

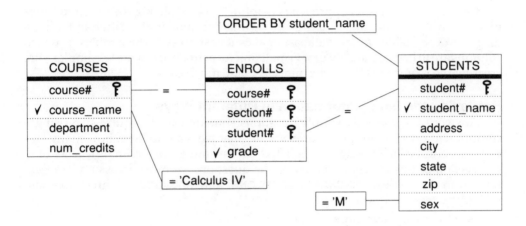

• SQL

```
SELECT course_name, student_name, grade
    FROM COURSES, ENROLLS, STUDENTS
    WHERE course_name = 'Calculus IV' AND
          sex = 'M' AND
          COURSES.course# = ENROLLS.course# AND
          ENROLLS.student# = STUDENTS.student#
    ORDER BY student_name;
```

• Results

course_name	student_name	grade
Calculus IV	John Anderson	4
Calculus IV	Bob Dawson	1

Joins With More Than Three Tables

A single query can access information stored in any number of tables within a database. Four, five, or more tables can be joined together, usually in combination with an appropriate **WHERE** clause, to retrieve the required information. In SQL, these larger joins are constructed just like those using only two or three tables. The only differences are the number of tables in the **FROM** clause and the complexity of the **WHERE** clause.

Once again, the visual approach is helpful. Since extracting the required information requires matching values from various columns in the different tables, a diagram of the tables in the database makes it easy to see which tables in which columns are to be matched. By first visualizing (or actually drawing) a complex join, creating the required SQL for the query is made much easier.

Retrieving the Same Information in Different Ways

Answering apparently simple questions sometimes can require surprisingly complicated queries. Suppose, for example, that we want to learn how many students are enrolled in Dr. Engle's English class (assuming that Dr. Engle teaches only one section of this course). To answer the question, we must access no less than three different tables: **TEACHERS**, **SECTIONS**, and **COURSES**. A three-table join which answers this question is

```
SELECT num_students
    FROM TEACHERS, SECTIONS, COURSES
    WHERE  TEACHERS.teacher_name = 'Dr. Engle' AND
           COURSES.course_name = 'English Composition' AND
           TEACHERS.teacher# = SECTIONS.teacher# AND
           SECTIONS.course# = COURSES.course#;
```

In our example database, however, there is another way to answer this same question. Using **COUNT**, and accessing information stored in four tables, we can retrieve the same information:

```
SELECT COUNT(student#)
    FROM COURSES, SECTIONS, ENROLLS, TEACHERS
    WHERE  course_name = 'English Composition' AND
           teacher_name =  'Dr. Engle' AND
           TEACHERS.teacher# = SECTIONS.teacher# AND
           COURSES.course# = SECTIONS.course# AND
           SECTIONS.course# = ENROLLS.course# AND
           SECTIONS.section# = ENROLLS.section#;
```

The result of both this and the previous query is a single value, indicating the number of students in Dr. Engle's English class.

A reasonable question to ask is, why bother to store the number of students in each class at all? Couldn't we dispense entirely with the column called **num_students** in the **SECTIONS** table? The answer is yes; that column contains information which we can always derive based on values stored in other tables. Nevertheless, storing such redundant information is sometimes a useful thing. In this database, for instance, it is reasonable to believe that many queries will request the number of students in a particular section of a course. To avoid the overhead of frequently performing the complex four-table join shown above, it may be worthwhile to store the information directly in its own column. A drawback of this choice, however, is that the **num_students** column must be updated each time a student is added to or deleted from a section of a course. Whether redundant columns such as this are included in a database is just one example of the kinds of decisions which must be made when designing a relational database.

Example: joins with four tables

• Problem

How many students are in Dr. Engle's English class?

• Query Diagram

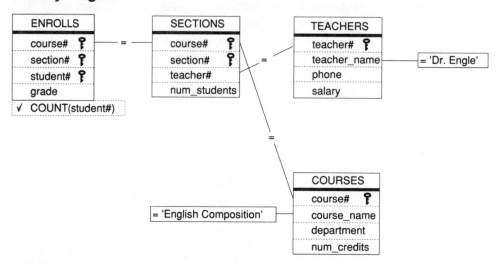

• SQL

```
SELECT COUNT(student#)
    FROM ENROLLS, SECTIONS, TEACHERS, COURSES
    WHERE teacher_name =  'Dr. Engle' AND
          course_name = 'English Composition' AND
          ENROLLS.course# = SECTIONS.course# AND
          SECTIONS.teacher# = TEACHERS.teacher# AND
          SECTIONS.course# = COURSES.course#;;
```

• Results

```
COUNT(student#)
```

                3

• Note

This query is slightly more powerful than the one discussed on the previous pages. Then, we assumed Dr. Engle taught only a single section of English Composition, and that assumption was built into the query. This query, on the other hand, returns the correct results whether Dr. Engle teaches one or more sections of English Composition.

Example: joins with four tables

• Problem

Produce a list of the names and addresses of Dr. Horn's students. Order the list alphabetically by student name.

• Query Diagram

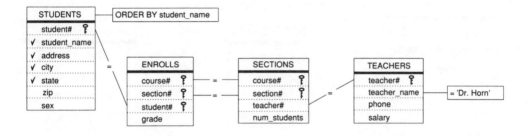

• SQL

```
SELECT student_name, address, city, state
    FROM STUDENTS, ENROLLS, SECTIONS, TEACHERS
    WHERE teacher_name = 'Dr. Horn' AND
          TEACHERS.teacher# = SECTIONS.teacher# AND
          SECTIONS.section# = ENROLLS.section# AND
          SECTIONS.course# = ENROLLS.course# AND
          ENROLLS.student# = STUDENTS.student#
    ORDER BY student_name;
```

• Results

student_name	address	city	state
Carol Dean	983 Park Avenue	Boston	MA
Janet Thomas	441 6th Street	Erie	PA

Example: joins with five tables

• Problem

Produce a roster for each course by teacher, listing the courses and sections they teach along with the names of all students enrolled in each.

• Query Diagram

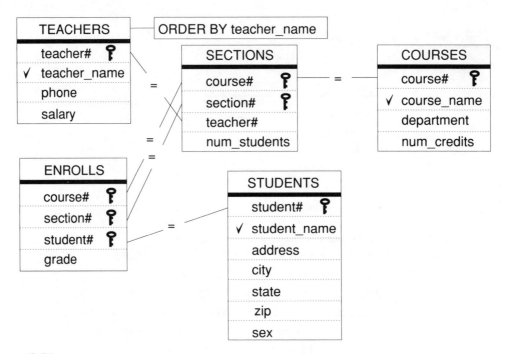

• SQL

```
SELECT teacher_name, course_name, student_name
    FROM TEACHERS, SECTIONS, COURSES, ENROLLS, STUDENTS
    WHERE TEACHERS.teacher# = SECTIONS.teacher# AND
        SECTIONS.course# = COURSES.course# AND
        SECTIONS.section# = ENROLLS.section# AND
        SECTIONS.course# = ENROLLS.course# AND
        ENROLLS.student# = STUDENTS.student#
    ORDER BY teacher_name;
```

• Results

teacher_name	course_name	student_name
Dr. Cooke	Compiler Writing	John Anderson
Dr. Cooke	Compiler Writing	Bill Jones
Dr. Engle	English Composition	Allen Thomas
Dr. Engle	English Composition	Joe Adams
Dr. Engle	English Composition	Howard Mansfield
Dr. Horn	Western Civilization	Janet Thomas
Dr. Horn	Western Civilization	Carol Dean
Dr. Lowe	Calculus IV	Carol Dean
Dr. Lowe	Calculus IV	Val Shipp
Dr. Lowe	Calculus IV	John Anderson
Dr. Lowe	Calculus IV	Susan Pugh
Dr. Lowe	Calculus IV	Bob Dawson
Dr. Lowe	Calculus IV	Susan Powell
Dr. Olsen	Western Civilization	Allen Thomas
Dr. Olsen	Western Civilization	Bob Dawson
Dr. Scango	Compiler Writing	Howard Mansfield
Dr. Scango	Compiler Writing	Carol Dean

Using GROUP BY in a Join

The **GROUP BY** clause is a powerful, but sometimes complex, part of SQL. When used in a join, both its power and its complexity are magnified.

Recall how **GROUP BY** works with single-table queries: the table is (conceptually) ordered according to the values of the column specified in the **GROUP BY** clause. All records that have the same value in that field comprise a single group. Next, the values of any specified aggregates are calculated for all of the records in each group. Finally, the results are printed, with one line for each group. And any column names specified after **SELECT** must either appear within an aggregate or in the **GROUP BY** clause itself.

These same basic rules apply to joins using **GROUP BY**. Suppose, for instance, that we wish to know the total number of students taught by each teacher. Answering this question requires information from both the **TEACHERS** table and the **SEC-TIONS** table, so a join is required. Since we want to look at students taught by each teacher, we must join the two tables using the **teacher#** column in each. Also, because we wish to learn the total number of students taught by each teacher, we can group the data by **teacher_name** and use **SUM** to add the groups. The resulting SQL query is

```
SELECT teacher_name, SUM(num_students)
    FROM TEACHERS, SECTIONS
    WHERE TEACHERS.teacher# = SECTIONS.teacher#
    GROUP BY teacher_name;
```

This query will (again conceptually) first perform the join, yielding only the selected columns from those records in the two tables where **TEACHERS.teacher#** = **SECTIONS.teacher#**. Next, these chosen records are ordered according to the values in their **teacher_name** field, and all records with the same value for **teacher_name** are assigned to a distinct group. Finally, the values in the **num_students** fields of the records in each group are added together, and the results are printed. (In the example database, each teacher teaches only one class. For this query, then, each group contains only a single record. If any teachers taught more than one class, their group would also contain more than one record.)

In general, **GROUP BY** in joins behaves just like **GROUP BY** in single-table queries. As in those simpler queries, a **HAVING** clause may also be specified to restrict the groups which are included in the query's results.

Example: using GROUP BY *in a join*

• Problem

What is the total number of students taught by each teacher?

• Query Diagram

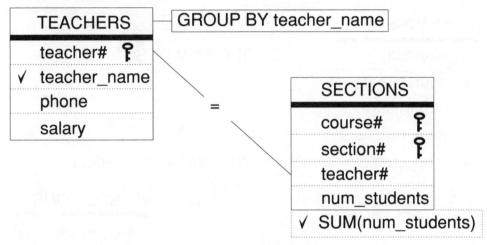

• SQL

```
SELECT teacher_name, SUM(num_students)
    FROM TEACHERS, SECTIONS
    WHERE TEACHERS.teacher# = SECTIONS.teacher#
    GROUP BY teacher_name;
```

• Results

teacher_name	SUM(num_students)
Dr. Cooke	3.00
Dr. Engle	3.00
Dr. Horn	2.00
Dr. Lowe	6.00
Dr. Olsen	2.00
Dr. Scango	2.00

Example: using GROUP BY *in a join*

• Problem

List in descending order the total number of credits awarded for each course.

• Query Diagram

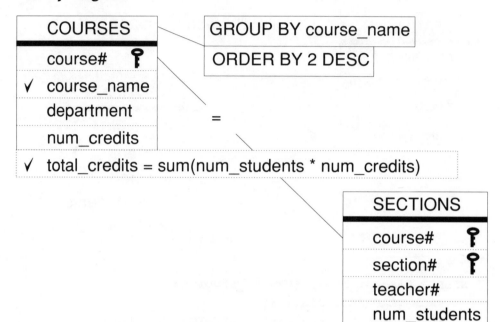

• SQL

```
SELECT course_name,
       total_credits = sum(num_students * num_credits)
   FROM COURSES, SECTIONS
   WHERE SECTIONS.course# = COURSES.course#
   GROUP BY course_name
   ORDER BY 2 DESC;
```

• Results

course_name	total_credits
Calculus IV	24.00
Compiler Writing	15.00
Western Civilization	12.00
English Composition	9.00

Example: using GROUP BY *in a join*

• Problem

How many students of each sex are enrolled in Calculus IV?

• Query Diagram

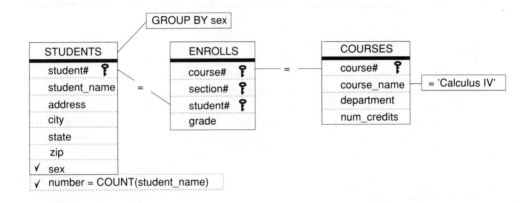

• SQL

```
SELECT sex, number = COUNT(student_name)
    FROM STUDENTS, ENROLLS, COURSES
    WHERE course_name = 'Calculus IV' AND
          COURSES.course# = ENROLLS.course# AND
          ENROLLS.student# = STUDENTS.student#
    GROUP BY sex;
```

• Results

sex	number
F	4
M	2

Queries Within Queries: Subqueries

6

A relational database consists entirely of tables. Every piece of information is stored in some column within one of the database's tables. SQL, since it is a query language for relational database systems, operates on these tables.

But you may already have noticed an interesting fact: the *results* of a SQL query are also a table. True, these tables are somewhat ephemeral, often existing only on a terminal screen. But even though a results table does not become part of the stored database, it, too, can be operated on via SQL queries. Performing this sort of access requires the use of *subqueries*.

What is a Subquery?

The result of every SQL query is a table. Sometimes, that table is very simple, containing only a single row and column (or even being entirely empty). In other cases, a results table may be much larger than any of the tables actually stored in the database. In either case, the table which results from executing one query (the subquery) can be the input for another query. It is even possible for the results of *that* query to be the input for yet another, and so on. In practice, though, queries are seldom nested more than two deep.

Many of the queries which we have already seen can be recast using subqueries. For some questions, including some apparently straightforward ones, using a subquery is the easiest route to the answer. For others, using a subquery is virtually a requirement.

Suppose we wish to know the names of all students who received a B (expressed numerically, a 3) in any of their classes. We could learn this with

```
SELECT DISTINCT student_name
    FROM STUDENTS, ENROLLS
    WHERE grade = 3 AND
            STUDENTS.student# = ENROLLS.student#;
```

(Since we want each selected student's name listed only once, and since some students may have received B's in two or more classes, this query uses the **DISTINCT** option.)

We could also answer this question using a subquery, like

```
SELECT DISTINCT student_name
    FROM STUDENTS
    WHERE student# IN
            (SELECT student#
                FROM ENROLLS
                WHERE grade = 3);
```

The query within parentheses is the subquery. When the entire query is executed, this subquery must be completed first. The result of the subquery is the following table:

student#

148
210
298
298
473
558

This table is then used as input to the **WHERE** clause in the main query. The condition expressed in that **WHERE** clause (**student# IN . . .**) will be true only for those records in the **STUDENTS** table whose **student#** is in the list above, the table returned by the subquery. Since the above table contains only the **student#**s of students who received a B, only the **student_name**s from those records in **STUDENTS** will appear in the results of the entire query. Note also that **DISTINCT** need not be used in this case, because of the way **IN** works: the **WHERE** clause is true for any **student#** that appears *at least once* in the result of the subquery. Even if the same **student#** appears more than once, as does the number 298 in the example above, that student's name will not appear more than once in the result of the entire query.

Subqueries can appear in **HAVING** clauses (and thus in **SELECT**s using **GROUP BY**) as well as in **WHERE** clauses. The rules are the same: the subquery is executed first, and its results are used as input to the condition specified in the **HAVING** clause. Like a **WHERE** clause, the **HAVING** clause then evaluates to either true or false.

According to the SQL standard, all subqueries must be surrounded by parentheses. As with so many parts of the standard, some implementations don't enforce this restriction. Using subqueries can become rather complicated, however, and so using clarifying parentheses is always a good idea.

Example: a simple subquery

• *Problem*

Which students received B's in any course?

• *Query Diagram*

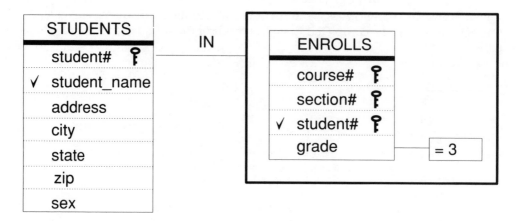

• *SQL*

```
SELECT student_name
    FROM STUDENTS
    WHERE student# IN
           (SELECT student#
               FROM ENROLLS
               WHERE grade = 3);
```

• *Results*

student_name

Susan Powell
Bob Dawson
Howard Mansfield
Carol Dean
Val Shipp

Using Comparison Operators With Subqueries

In Chapter 3, we described the various comparison operators available in SQL: =, <>, <, >, <=, and >=. All of these can also be used with subqueries. In addition, the **IN** and **NOT IN** keywords may be used.

We have already seen an example using **IN**. **NOT IN** is used with subqueries in an analogous way to **IN**. With **NOT IN**, however, the **WHERE** clause is true if and only if the desired values are *not* found in the table resulting from execution of the subquery.

Using the comparison operators is more problematic. Consider how = is used in

```
SELECT student_name
    FROM STUDENTS
    WHERE student# =
            (SELECT student#
                FROM ENROLLS
                WHERE grade = 1);
```

As it happens, this query will work as expected, and return the **student_name** of the one student in our example database who received a D (or numerically, a 1). But suppose that more than one student had received a D? Or suppose we had entered this same query, but asked about B's instead of D's?

In this case, SQL is faced with the impossible task of comparing a single value to a table full of values. The exact results of such a query vary from system to system, but in general, the = operator should not be used with subqueries unless you know in advance that the result of the subquery is a table with only one record. When you don't know this (which is most of the time), use **IN**. The effect is the same, but the subquery is allowed to return a table with multiple values.

Using <> with subqueries causes similar problems. Instead of this potentially troublesome comparison operator, then, it is usually simpler to achieve the same effect by using **NOT IN**.

The other comparison operators, including <, >, <=, and >=, also can't be used alone unless the subquery will return only a single value. Unlike = and <>, however, there is no simple substitute. (They can, however, be used in conjunction with **ANY** and **ALL**, as described in the next section.)

Nevertheless, subqueries that are guaranteed to return only a single value are not that unusual, so the comparison operators are still useful on their own in some cases. Since a subquery can use aggregates like any other query, we could see, for instance, which teachers earn a lower than average salary with

```
SELECT teacher_name
    FROM TEACHERS
    WHERE salary <
            (SELECT AVG(salary)
                FROM TEACHERS);
```

This query will return the **teacher_name**s of only those teachers whose salaries are below the average. Note that since aggregates like **AVG** can't appear in a **WHERE** clause, the simplest way to answer this question is with a subquery.

Similarly, to retrieve information about sections with enrollments greater than average, we could type

```
SELECT course#, section#, num_students
   FROM SECTIONS
   WHERE num_students >
           (SELECT AVG(num_students)
           FROM SECTIONS);
```

In both cases, the table resulting from execution of the parenthesized subquery contains only a single value, and therefore is fair game to be used immediately following a comparison operator.

It is also possible to use **AND**, **OR**, and **NOT** in a **WHERE** clause involving subqueries. In fact, a single query can tie together two or more subqueries using these constructs. More commonly, though, a **WHERE** clause will combine a subquery and some more common condition, such as a test for equality, in a single query.

Example: a subquery using the comparison <

• *Problem*

Which teachers earn less than average?

• *Query Diagram*

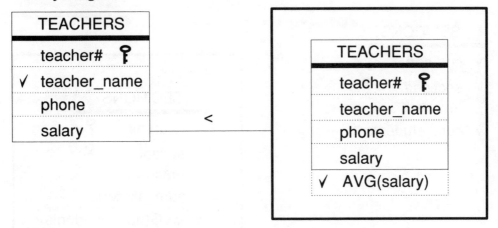

• *SQL*

```
SELECT teacher_name
    FROM TEACHERS
    WHERE salary <
          (SELECT AVG(salary)
              FROM TEACHERS);
```

• *Results*

```
teacher_name
```

```
Dr. Horn
Dr. Lowe
Dr. Cooke
```

Example: a subquery using the comparison >

• *Problem*

Which sections have more than the average number of students?

• *Query Diagram*

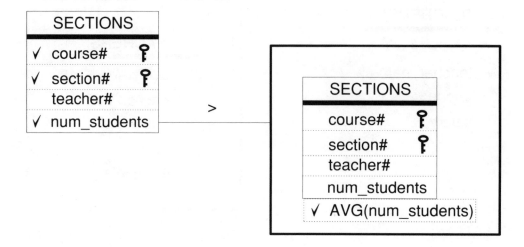

•*SQL*

```
SELECT course#, section#, num_students
   FROM SECTIONS
   WHERE num_students >
         (SELECT AVG(num_students)
            FROM SECTIONS);
```

• *Results*

course#	section#	num_students
730	1	6

Using ANY and ALL

As was just described, a subquery which immediately follows one of the comparison operators is expected to return only a single value. It is possible, however, to use comparison operators with subqueries returning multiple values by following the operator with either of the words **ANY** or **ALL**.

When **ANY** is used, the **WHERE** or **HAVING** clause containing the subquery will be true if the specified operator is true for *any* of the values returned by the subquery. In other words, if the expression containing the operator is true for at least one of the values returned by the subquery, the entire **WHERE** or **HAVING** clause will be true. (The SQL standard also allows the word **SOME** to be used as a synonym for **ANY**, with no change in meaning. Once again, however, not all implementations of SQL support this substitution.) For example, we could say

```
SELECT student_name
    FROM STUDENTS
    WHERE student# = ANY
            (SELECT student#
                FROM ENROLLS
                WHERE grade = 3);
```

The result of this query will be the names of all students who received at least one B. Because the subquery will return more than one value, we could not use the = operator by itself. Following it with **ANY**, however, allows us to compare the **student#** from **STUDENTS** with each of the results of the subquery.

When used to test for equality, using **ANY** is exactly equivalent to using **IN**. Therefore, the query

```
SELECT student_name
    FROM STUDENTS
    WHERE student# IN
            (SELECT student#
                FROM ENROLLS
                WHERE grade = 3);
```

will return results identical to those of the previous example. With the other comparison operators, however, **ANY** can be a useful addition, since it allows comparisons against subqueries which return more than one value.

For example, to see the names of students whose average grade is higher than that of the student with the lowest average grade (and to provide an example of a **HAVING** clause containing a subquery), we could type

```
SELECT student_name, AVG(grade)
    FROM STUDENTS, ENROLLS
    WHERE STUDENTS.student# = ENROLLS.student#
    GROUP BY student_name
    HAVING AVG(grade) > ANY
            (SELECT AVG(grade)
                FROM ENROLLS
                GROUP BY student#);
```

The result of the subquery is a table containing the average grade of every student (note that this is not the same as the student's grade point average, or GPA, since the number of credits given for each course is not included in this calculation). The outer query also calculates every student's average grade, but relies on the subquery within its **HAVING** clause to determine which of those students' names and average grades appear in its results. Only those students whose average grade is greater than at least one other student's average grade will be selected. In other words, this query will list the names of all students except those with the lowest average grade.

ALL works in an analogous fashion. Preceding a subquery with some comparison operator and the word **ALL** means that the **WHERE** or **HAVING** clause containing the subquery will be true only if the comparison is true for *all* values returned by the subquery. For example, to see the names of all students who received a grade in some course that equaled or exceeded the highest all-around average grade, one could type

```
SELECT DISTINCT student_name, grade
    FROM STUDENTS, ENROLLS
    WHERE STUDENTS.student# = ENROLLS.student# AND
            grade >= ALL
            (SELECT AVG(grade)
             FROM ENROLLS
             GROUP BY student#);
```

The result of this query would be the names and grades of students meeting the requirement specified above. Because a single student may have received a qualifying grade in more than one class, **DISTINCT** is used to cause that student's name to appear only once in the query's results.

Example: a subquery using ANY

• *Problem*

Which students received B's in any course?

• *Query Diagram*

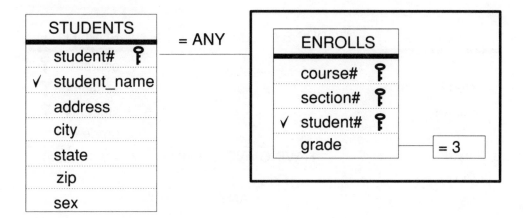

• *SQL*

```
SELECT student_name
    FROM STUDENTS
    WHERE student# = ANY
            (SELECT student#
                FROM ENROLLS
                WHERE grade = 3);
```

• *Results*

student_name

Susan Powell
Bob Dawson
Howard Mansfield
Carol Dean
Val Shipp

Example: a subquery using ANY

• *Problem*

List all students whose average grade is greater than the lowest average grade.

• *Query Diagram*

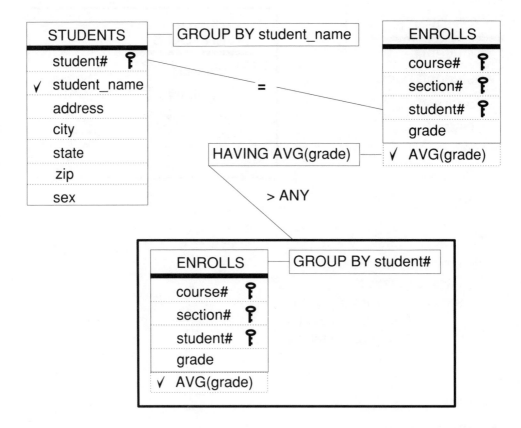

• *SQL*

```
SELECT student_name, AVG(grade)
   FROM STUDENTS, ENROLLS
   WHERE STUDENTS.student# = ENROLLS.student#
   GROUP BY student_name
   HAVING AVG(grade) > ANY
          (SELECT AVG(grade)
              FROM ENROLLS
              GROUP BY student#);
```

• Results

student_name	AVG(grade)
Allen Thomas	2.00
Bill Jones	2.00
Bob Dawson	2.00
Howard Mansfield	3.00
Janet Thomas	4.00
Joe Adams	4.00
John Anderson	4.00
Susan Powell	3.00
Susan Pugh	2.00
Val Shipp	3.00

Example: a subquery using ALL

• Problem

List the names and grades of students who received some grade greater than or equal to the highest all-around average grade.

• Query Diagram

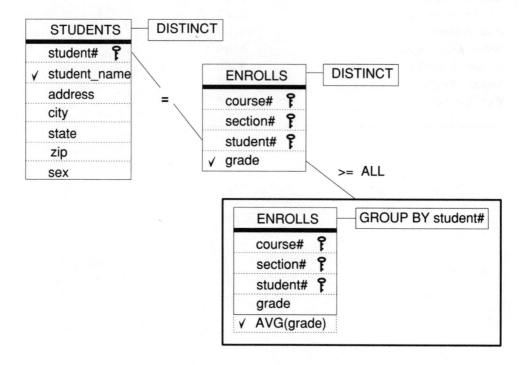

• SQL

```
SELECT DISTINCT student_name, grade
   FROM STUDENTS, ENROLLS
   WHERE STUDENTS.student# = ENROLLS.student# AND
         grade >= ALL
         (SELECT AVG(grade)
          FROM ENROLLS
          GROUP BY student#);
```

• *Results*

student_name	grade
Joe Adams	4
John Anderson	4
Janet Thomas	4

Existence Tests

All subqueries return a table, which is then used as input to the **WHERE** clause in the enclosing query. So far, we have been concerned with comparing the actual values in this returned table to other values, using operators like **=**, **>**, and **<**. As always, the records for which the **WHERE** clause was true were selected. SQL also allows us to test not just the values contained in records returned by a subquery, but the existence or non-existence of any such records as well. For this, the language provides **EXISTS** and **NOT EXISTS**.

Recall that each part of a **WHERE** clause is either true or false for each record in the table. A subquery preceded by the word **EXISTS** will be true if the subquery returns any records at all, regardless of the value of those records (even a record containing all **NULL**s qualifies). Similarly, a subquery preceded by **NOT EXISTS** will be true if the subquery returns no records, i.e., an empty table with no rows and no columns.

Existence tests, although conceptually very simple, can be quite useful. Their most common use, however, is in correlated subqueries, described next.

Correlated Subqueries

In the examples shown so far, the subquery is first evaluated, and then the table resulting from that evaluation is used as input to the main query. SQL also allows subqueries to be evaluated multiple times, once for each record accessed by the main query. Such subqueries are called *correlated subqueries*.

Suppose, for example, that we wished to find the names and student numbers of any students who are not currently enrolled in any classes. One way to express this request in SQL is

```
SELECT student#, student_name
    FROM STUDENTS S
    WHERE NOT EXISTS
            (SELECT *
                FROM ENROLLS E
                WHERE E.student# = S.student#);
```

Unlike the earlier examples, the parenthesized subquery here is not executed just once. Instead, this subquery is executed once for *each* record in the **STUDENTS** table. For each execution, the value of the **student#** field from a record in **STUDENTS** is compared with the value of **student#** from *every* record in **ENROLLS** (via the condition **E.student# = S.student#** in the subquery's **WHERE** clause). Whenever the two **student#**'s match, the subquery adds that record from **ENROLLS** to its result table.

Recall from the last section how **NOT EXISTS** works: if the table returned by the subquery is not empty, i.e., if it contains at least one record, the **NOT EXISTS** condition is false. If, however, the table returned by the subquery is empty, i.e., if it contains no records, the **NOT EXISTS** condition is true. In the example above, the subquery compares the **student#** field of each record in **STUDENTS** with every **student#** field in the **ENROLLS** table. If at least one match is found, then this student is enrolled in some course, the table resulting from the subquery will not be empty, and the **NOT EXISTS** condition will be false. If no matches are found, however, then the subquery will return an empty table, the **NOT EXISTS** condition will be true, and the **student_name** and **student#** fields of the current record in the main query will be selected.

Note that the alias **S** is defined for the **STUDENTS** table in the main query, and that that alias is used within the subquery. Note also that the value of **S.student#**, which changes each time the subquery is executed, is taken from (or correlated with) the current record in the main query. It is from this relationship that the term "correlated subquery" is derived. To recognize correlated subqueries, look for the use within the subquery of an alias (or, occasionally, of a complete table name) defined only in the main query.

The above example could also have been written without the alias name for **EN-ROLLS** and with only one qualified name, like

```
SELECT student#, student_name
    FROM STUDENTS S
    WHERE NOT EXISTS
           (SELECT *
               FROM ENROLLS
               WHERE student# = S.student#);
```

Again, **S.student#** takes its value from the current record in **STUDENTS**. The reference to **student#** in the subquery's **WHERE** clause still refers to that column in the **ENROLLS** table; in the absence of a qualified name, the column is assumed to come from the "nearest" table. In this case, that table is **ENROLLS**. The results of this query are identical to those of the one shown previously.

Correlated subqueries can also be used with comparison operators, **ANY** and **ALL**, and **EXISTS**. For instance, to see which students received a grade higher than the average in their section, and to order the results by course number, one could type

```
SELECT student_name, grade, course#, section#
    FROM STUDENTS, ENROLLS E
    WHERE STUDENTS.student# = E.student# AND
           grade >
           (SELECT AVG(grade)
               FROM ENROLLS
               WHERE course# = E.course# AND
                       section# = E.section#)
    ORDER BY course#;
```

Unlike the previous example, the main query accesses two different tables. Conceptually, this query is processed as follows: first, the join of **STUDENTS** and **ENROLLS** is formed, a table containing all possible combinations of records from the two tables. Then, only those records in which **STUDENTS.student#** = **ENROLLS.student#** are selected. For each of these records, the subquery is executed, returning the average grade for the course and section associated with the current record from the **ENROLLS** table. If the grade in that record is greater than this average, the main query's **WHERE** clause is true, and the **student_name**, **grade**, **course#**, and **section#** of that record is selected. Finally, all selected records are ordered by the value in their **course#** field.

Using HAVING With Correlated Subqueries

The **HAVING** clause was discussed in the context of **GROUP BY** in Chapter 4. **HAVING** is also useful with correlated subqueries. While a **WHERE** clause specifies restrictions that individual records must meet to be selected, a **HAVING** clause places a restriction on the results of an entire query (or, when used with **GROUP BY**, of a group). When used without **GROUP BY**, a **HAVING** clause can prevent a query from returning anything at all.

To see why this is useful, suppose we wanted to know which students are taking more than two courses. One way to express this in SQL is

```
SELECT student_name
    FROM STUDENTS S
    WHERE EXISTS
            (SELECT COUNT(*)
                FROM ENROLLS
                WHERE student# = S.student#
                HAVING COUNT(*) > 2);
```

As before, the subquery will be executed once for each record in the **STUDENTS** table (we know this because of the reference to the alias **S** within the subquery). And as always, the **student_name** field from the current **STUDENTS** record will be selected whenever the main query's **WHERE** clause is true. The question to be answered, then, is when will this **WHERE** clause be true?

Once again, the **EXISTS** operation (and thus the main query's **WHERE** clause) returns true if and only if the subquery returns a non-empty table, i.e., a table with at least one row and column. Without the **HAVING** clause, the subquery would return the number of courses in which each student was enrolled. The effect of the **HAVING** clause, however, is to eliminate entirely the results of any subquery executions which return two or fewer records. Once again, since a **HAVING** clause (without **GROUP BY**) places a restriction on the query as a whole, any query which would otherwise return less than three records will now return an empty table. The **EXISTS** in the main query, and thus the main query's **WHERE** clause, will therefore be true only for those students who are enrolled in more than two courses.

Example: a correlated subquery using NOT EXISTS

• Problem

Which students are not enrolled in any courses?

• Query Diagram

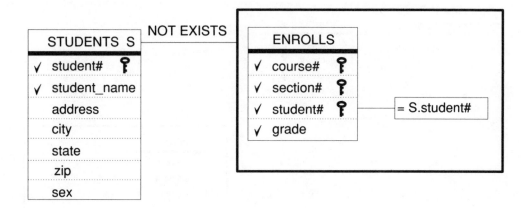

• SQL

```
SELECT student#, student_name
   FROM STUDENTS S
   WHERE NOT EXISTS
        (SELECT *
            FROM ENROLLS
            WHERE student# = S.student#);
```

• Results

```
student# student_name
_____

    354   Janet Ladd
_____
```

Example: a correlated subquery using >

• *Problem*

Which students received a grade higher than the average in their section?

• *Query Diagram*

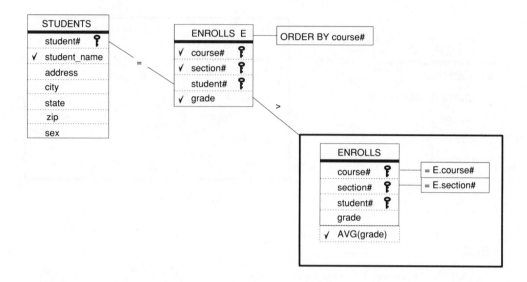

• *SQL*

```
SELECT student_name, grade, course#, section#
    FROM STUDENTS, ENROLLS E
    WHERE STUDENTS.student# = E.student# AND
        grade >
        (SELECT AVG(grade)
            FROM ENROLLS
            WHERE course# = E.course# AND
                section# = E.section#)
    ORDER BY course#;
```

• *Results*

student_name	grade	course#	section#
Joe Adams	4	290	1
Janet Thomas	4	450	1
John Anderson	4	480	1
Howard Mansfield	3	480	2
Susan Powell	3	730	1
John Anderson	4	730	1
Val Shipp	3	730	1
Carol Dean	3	730	1

Example: a correlated subquery using `ALL`

• *Problem*

Which courses have only male students?

• *Query Diagram*

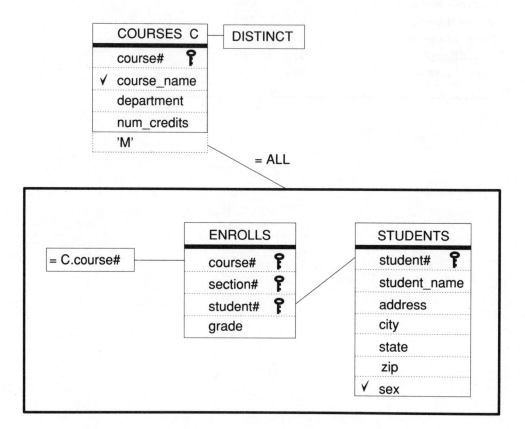

• *SQL*

```
SELECT DISTINCT course_name
    FROM COURSES C
    WHERE 'M' = ALL
            (SELECT sex
                FROM ENROLLS, STUDENTS
                WHERE ENROLLS.student# =
                        STUDENTS.student# AND
                        ENROLLS.course# = C.course#);
```

• *Results*

```
course_name
```
_____

```
English Composition
```
_____

• *Note*

This example introduces another new idea: comparing the results returned by a subquery to a constant value. In this case, the constant is the single character 'M', indicated by the temporary column shown in the **COURSES** table. In general, SQL allows a constant to appear wherever a column name can appear, as long as the constant is a value of the correct type.

Example: a correlated subquery using EXISTS *and* HAVING

• Problem

Which students are taking more than 2 courses?

• Query Diagram

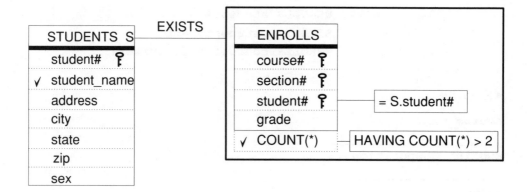

• SQL

```
SELECT student_name
    FROM STUDENTS S
    WHERE EXISTS
            (SELECT COUNT(*)
                FROM ENROLLS
                WHERE student# = S.student#
                HAVING COUNT(*) > 2);
```

• Results

student_name

_____

Carol Dean

_____

Example: a correlated subquery using EXISTS *and* HAVING

• *Problem*

List the departments that have courses with more than 4 students.

• *Query Diagram*

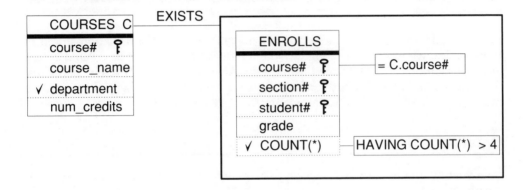

• *SQL*

```
SELECT department
    FROM COURSES C
    WHERE EXISTS
            (SELECT COUNT(*)
                FROM ENROLLS
                WHERE course# = C.course#
                HAVING COUNT(*) > 4);
```

• *Results*

department

_____

Math
Computer Science

_____

Creating and Destroying Tables

7

Relational databases consist solely of tables. To retrieve the information stored in those tables, we can use the **SELECT** statement. But tables must be created before any information can be retrieved from them. Also, it may sometimes be necessary to destroy existing tables in the database. To carry out these essential actions, we must introduce two new SQL statements: **CREATE** and **DROP**.

Creating a Table

Creating a table with SQL is easy. The general form of a SQL statement that creates a table is

```
CREATE TABLE <table>
    (<column descriptions>);
```

The first two words of the statement, **CREATE TABLE**, tell SQL what we are doing. Next comes **<table>**, the name we want to give this newly created table (as always, expressions using **<** and **>** are replaced by actual words in SQL statements). Finally come the **<column descriptions>**, a parenthesized list giving the name and type of each column we want to be in the table.

For example, the **STUDENTS** table from the example database might have been created by typing

```
CREATE TABLE STUDENTS
    (student# SMALLINT,
     student_name CHAR (18),
     address CHAR (20),
     city CHAR (10),
     state CHAR (2),
     zip CHAR (5),
     sex CHAR (1) );
```

This statement creates a table called **STUDENTS** with seven columns. The first column of this table contains values of type **SMALLINT**, while all the others contain character strings of various lengths. After this statement is executed, the **STUDENTS** table exists, but it contains no records.

The numbers in parentheses after the word **CHAR** indicate the maximum length of a character string value which can be stored in that column. Given the definition above, the **STUDENTS** table can't store student names longer than 18 characters, because the **student_name** column is defined as **CHAR (18)**. Similarly, an address of more than 20 characters and a zip of more than 5 characters are prohibited. (Recall that different implementations of SQL allow different types of information in their tables' columns—for a review of those allowed by the SQL standard, turn back to Chapter 2).

As usual, where line breaks occur makes no difference, except possibly to a human reader. This entire **CREATE** statement could have appeared on one line, and the effect would have been the same. Also, some of the spaces in the above example are added only for readability and have no effect on the execution of the statement. While the space between **student_name** and **CHAR** is required (how else could SQL tell where the column name left off and the type began?), the space between **CHAR** and **(18)** is not. While including that space may make the statement more readable, the result would have been identical had it read **CHAR(18)**.

Another example: the **TEACHERS** table. To create this table, one could type

```
CREATE TABLE TEACHERS
    (teacher# SMALLINT,
     teacher_name CHAR (18),
     phone CHAR (10),
     salary FLOAT);
```

Again, the column names are listed along with their type following the new table's name. Along with a **SMALLINT** and two **CHAR** columns, the **TEACHERS** table stores salaries in a column of type **FLOAT**. As before, limits must be specified for the character strings. In this table, teacher names can't exceed 18 characters, and teacher phone numbers can't contain more than 10.

Unlike **SELECT**, execution of a **CREATE** does not return results to the user. Since **CREATE** does not choose values from existing tables, but instead creates an entirely new table, there are no results to return. Most implementations of SQL will respond, however, with a statement indicating that the specified table was created.

The SQL standard defines no way to change a table's structure once it is created. Some implementations of SQL, such as those found in ORACLE and IBM's DB2, include an **ALTER** statement, which allows the structure of an existing table to be modified. Check the documentation for the system you are using to see if and how this can be done in your environment.

Disallowing NULL Values

If desired, we can specify during creation that one or more columns may not contain **NULL** values. To do this, the words **NOT NULL** may be added following the type of any column. If this is done, SQL won't allow a **NULL** value to appear in that column of the table.

For example, to require that no student numbers be **NULL**, we could modify the **CREATE** statement for the **STUDENT** table to read

```
CREATE TABLE STUDENTS
   (student# SMALLINT NOT NULL,
    student_name CHAR (18),
    address CHAR (20),
    city CHAR (10),
    state CHAR (2),
    zip CHAR (5),
    sex CHAR (1) );
```

The result is just like before: a new table with seven columns. The only difference is that **NULL** values will not be allowed in the **student#** column.

Requiring Unique Values in a Column

It is also possible to specify at creation time that any column in a table may not contain duplicate values. If the **STUDENTS** table, for example, should contain one record for each student, and if each student is assigned a unique student number, then this table's **student#** column should never contain the same value twice. We can require this by specifying the keyword **UNIQUE** in the definition of this column. (Many systems, including DB2, do not yet support this aspect of the standard. Instead, they require specification of uniqueness when an *index* is created for that column in the table. Indexes, unique and otherwise, are described in Chapter 11.)

To modify the query above once again, we could type

```
CREATE TABLE STUDENTS
   (student# SMALLINT NOT NULL UNIQUE,
    student_name CHAR (18),
    address CHAR (20),
    city CHAR (10),
    state CHAR (2),
    zip CHAR (5),
    sex CHAR (1) );
```

If the **STUDENTS** table is created with this statement, SQL will not allow the same value to appear twice in the table's **student#** column. Any attempt to violate this constraint will result in an error message from SQL.

Clearly, this constraint is not always useful. If the **sex** column were declared **UNIQUE**, for example, only one student of each sex would be allowed—a severe and irrational restriction. In some cases, however, requiring that a column contain unique values can be very useful.

An important point about **UNIQUE**: any column declared to be **UNIQUE** must also be declared as **NOT NULL**. It is not possible to define a column which must contain unique values, but may also contain **NULL**s. SQL will return an error message if you attempt to create a table with such a column.

If more than one column is to contain unique values, the SQL standard allows specifying those unique columns at the end of the **CREATE** statement. For example, if all teachers are required to have both unique teacher numbers and unique phone numbers, the table could be created with

```
CREATE TABLE TEACHERS
     (teacher# SMALLINT NOT NULL,
      teacher_name CHAR (18),
      phone CHAR (10) NOT NULL,
      salary FLOAT,
      UNIQUE(teacher#, phone) );
```

In this variant, the names of the columns required to contain unique values are listed together in parentheses at the end of the **CREATE**. Note that, as SQL requires, both columns are also declared as **NOT NULL**.

This form of **UNIQUE** is not special in any way. The exact same effect could have been achieved with

```
CREATE TABLE TEACHERS
     (teacher# SMALLINT NOT NULL UNIQUE,
      teacher_name CHAR (18),
      phone CHAR (10) NOT NULL UNIQUE,
      salary FLOAT);
```

Recall that the values to be used as keys in a table must be unique. Also, it makes no sense to allow **NULL** values within keys. Therefore, if a column's values are to be used as keys, that column should be declared **NOT NULL UNIQUE** when the table is created. In other words, no key column should be allowed to contain duplicate values, and the value **NULL** should never appear in that column.

Example: creating a table

• Problem

Create the **STUDENTS** table.

• Query Diagram

STUDENTS		
student#	SMALLINT	—— NOT NULL UNIQUE
student_name	CHAR(18)	
address	CHAR(20)	
city	CHAR(10)	
state	CHAR(2)	
zip	CHAR(5)	
sex	CHAR(1)	

• SQL

```
CREATE TABLE STUDENTS
    (student# SMALLINT NOT NULL UNIQUE,
     student_name CHAR (18),
     address CHAR (20),
     city CHAR (10),
     state CHAR (2),
     zip CHAR (5),
     sex CHAR (1) );
```

Example: creating a table

• Problem

Create the **TEACHERS** table.

• Query Diagram

```
              TEACHERS
   ┌──────────────────────────────┐
   │                              │
   ├──────────────────────────────┤
   │ teacher#       SMALLINT      │───── NOT NULL UNIQUE
   │ teacher_name   CHAR(18)      │
   │ phone          CHAR(10)      │
   │ salary         FLOAT         │
   └──────────────────────────────┘
```

• SQL

```
CREATE TABLE TEACHERS
    (teacher# SMALLINT NOT NULL UNIQUE,
     teacher_name CHAR (18),
     phone CHAR (10),
     salary FLOAT);
```

Example: creating a table

• *Problem*

Create the **ENROLLS** table.

• *Query Diagram*

ENROLLS		
course#	SMALLINT	NOT NULL UNIQUE
section#	SMALLINT	NOT NULL UNIQUE
student#	SMALLINT	NOT NULL UNIQUE
grade	SMALLINT	

• *SQL*

```
CREATE TABLE ENROLLS
    (course# SMALLINT NOT NULL UNIQUE,
     section# SMALLINT NOT NULL UNIQUE,
     student# SMALLINT NOT NULL UNIQUE,
     grade SMALLINT);
```

Example: creating a table

• Problem

Create the **COURSES** table.

• Query Diagram

• SQL

```
CREATE TABLE COURSES
    (course# SMALLINT NOT NULL UNIQUE,
     course_name CHAR (20),
     department CHAR (16),
     num_credits SMALLINT);
```

Example: creating a table

• Problem

Create the **SECTIONS** table.

• Query Diagram

SECTIONS		
course#	SMALLINT	NOT NULL UNIQUE
section#	SMALLINT	NOT NULL UNIQUE
teacher#	SMALLINT	
num_students	SMALLINT	

• SQL

```
CREATE TABLE SECTIONS
    (course#  SMALLINT NOT NULL UNIQUE,
     section# SMALLINT NOT NULL UNIQUE,
     teacher# SMALLINT,
     num_students SMALLINT);
```

Destroying (Dropping) Tables

Just as SQL allows new tables to be created, it must provide a way to destroy existing tables. Oddly enough, the SQL standard does not define any mechanism for getting rid of existing tables. Virtually all SQL implementations, however, perform this function via the **DROP** statement.

The general form of **DROP** is

```
DROP TABLE <table>;
```

The first two words describe what is to be done, while the last, **<table>**, names the table to be deleted. Like **CREATE**, **DROP** returns no results other than a message from SQL indicating that the specified table has been destroyed. In some systems, all records must be deleted from a table before it can be dropped (destroyed). (Records are deleted from a table using the **DELETE** statement, described in the next chapter.) In others, dropping a table automatically deletes all of its records.

For example, to drop the **STUDENTS** table (assuming, perhaps, that all of its records had first been deleted), one could type

```
DROP TABLE STUDENTS;
```

Similarly, to drop an empty **TEACHERS** table, the command is

```
DROP TABLE TEACHERS;
```

Example: destroying (dropping) a table

• Problem

Drop the **STUDENTS** table.

• Query Diagram

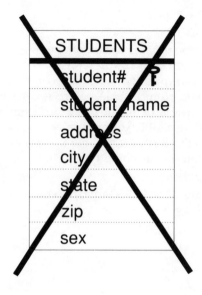

• SQL

```
DROP TABLE STUDENTS;
```

Example: destroying (dropping) a table

• Problem

Drop the **TEACHERS** table.

• Query Diagram

• SQL

```
DROP TABLE TEACHERS;
```

Adding, Modifying, and Deleting Records

8

As seen in the previous chapter, SQL's **CREATE** statement allows us to add new tables to our database. **CREATE** alone, however, does not provide any mechanism for populating our new tables with records. And while the **SELECT** statement allows us to access the records stored in a table, it does not let us add new records, delete old ones, or modify existing ones. To perform these functions, we must make use of still more SQL statements.

Adding Records to a Table

Once created, a new table must be filled with values. Because all values in a table are contained in records, adding a new value to a table requires adding an entire record. The SQL statement used to add a record is **INSERT**.

The general form of an **INSERT** statement is

```
INSERT INTO <table>(<column names>)
    VALUES (<values>);
```

This statement adds one record to the table specified by **<table>**. The new record may contain values for all or only some of its fields. Especially when only some of the new record's fields are given values, the names of those field's columns may optionally be specified via **<column names>** following the table's name. Next comes the keyword **VALUES** and the actual **<values>** of the record being added.

For example, to add Dr. Horn's record to the **TEACHERS** table, one could type either

```
INSERT INTO TEACHERS
    (teacher#, teacher_name, phone, salary)
    VALUES (303,
            'Dr. Horn',
            '257-3049',
            27540.00);
```

or just

```
INSERT INTO TEACHERS
    VALUES (303,
            'Dr. Horn',
            '257-3049',
            27540.00);
```

Either statement adds a single record containing the specified values for **teacher#**, **teacher_name**, **phone**, and **salary**, the four columns defined for the **TEACHERS** table. As usual in SQL, whether the new record's values are listed each on their own line, as shown above, or all on the same line makes no difference. And like **CREATE**, **INSERT** returns no results, with the possible exception of a message indicating the successful addition of a record to the table.

Whenever a new record is added, it is required that the data type of each value being added must match the type declared for that column when the table was created. For instance, it is not possible to insert a new record into the **TEACHERS** table with a value of 'None' for **teacher#**, since 'None' is a **CHAR** value, while **teacher#** was declared to be **SMALLINT**.

Recall that the records in a table are not ordered. In other words, a record is either in the table or not, but it is not meaningful to ask whether that record appears before or after some other record in the table. When a new record is added to a table using **INSERT**, then, that record is not necessarily added after the former "last" record nor before the former "first" one. It simply becomes a new member of the unordered list of records comprising that table.

As shown above, the **(<column names>)** may or may not be specified, since the record being added contains a value for all four columns, specified in the same order in which those columns were defined. It is possible (although usually not advisable) to specify a record's values in some other order. In this case, the names of the columns *must* be listed to tell SQL which value belongs to which column. In the absence of this list of names, as in the second example above, SQL assumes that the values are entered in order. For instance, the record in the **COURSES** table describing Calculus IV could have been added with

```
INSERT INTO COURSES
    (course_name, department, course#, num_credits)
    VALUES ('Calculus IV',
            'Math',
            730,
            4);
```

In this table, the columns were created in the order **course#**, **course_name**, **department**, **num_credits**. To specify the new record's values in some other order, that new order must be given. Of course, the ordering of the columns in **COURSES** does not change; the list of column names given in **INSERT** serves only to tell SQL which values belong to which fields in the new record.

Adding Records With Values Only For Some Columns

What happens if we don't specify values for all of the fields in a newly added record? What is the result, for instance, of saying

```
INSERT INTO STUDENTS
    (student#, student_name, city, state, sex)
    VALUES (558,
            'Val Shipp',
            'Chicago',
            'IL',
            'F');
```

As the list of column names indicates, we are specifying values only for the **student#**, **student_name**, **city**, **state**, and **sex** fields of this new record. What values are placed in the fields for which we have *not* specified values, **address** and **zip**? The answer should not be a surprise. Because every field in every record must have some value, and because we have not specified a value for those fields, SQL will place **NULL**s in both of them. When a record is inserted, any fields for which no value is given will automatically be set to **NULL**. Note that if an **INSERT** statement does not specify a value for a field whose column was declared as **NOT NULL** when the table was created, SQL will not allow the record to be added.

Example: adding a record to a table

• Problem

Add Dr. Horn's record to the **TEACHERS** table.

• Query Diagram

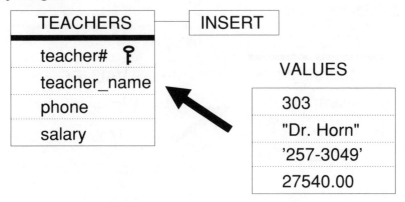

• SQL

```
INSERT INTO TEACHERS
    VALUES (303,
            'Dr. Horn',
            '257-3049',
            27540.00);
```

Example: adding a record to a table

• Problem

Add a record describing Calculus IV to the **COURSES** table, specifying the new values in a different order from that of the table's columns.

• Query Diagram

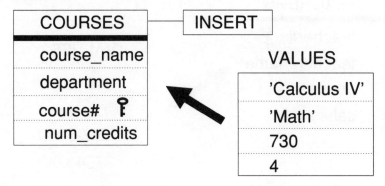

• SQL

```
INSERT INTO COURSES
    (course_name,department,course#, num_credits)
    VALUES ('Calculus IV',
            'Math',
            730,
            4);
```

Adding Records Using SELECT

SQL allows a second style of **INSERT**. The general form of this style is

```
INSERT INTO <table>(<column names>)
    SELECT <column names>
        FROM <table>
        WHERE <predicate>;
```

In place of the word **VALUE** and a list of values, this second form of **INSERT** includes a **SELECT** statement. This **SELECT** can be as simple or as complex as desired (and as always with simple **SELECT**s, the **WHERE** clause may be omitted).

With this second style of **INSERT**, the new values for a table are not directly specified by the user. Instead, they must be drawn from one or more tables which already exist in the database. For example, suppose we wished to promote all students who had received an A in any class to teachers. That is, the record in the **STUDENTS** table for any student who has received an A in one or more classes should be added to the **TEACHERS** table. (This is admittedly a very loose criterion for promotion to teacherhood.) An obvious problem: the columns in the two tables are not identical. The records in **TEACHERS** each have a **teacher#**, **teacher_name**, **phone**, and **salary**. Those in **STUDENTS**, on the other hand, contain fields for **student#**, **student_name**, **address**, and so on. To allow this promotion, we will assume that the selected students' **student#** and **student_name** fields will become the **teacher#** and **teacher_name** fields in the new record in **TEACHERS**. The other columns in **TEACHERS**, **phone** and **salary**, will simply be left unspecified.

To perform this operation, we must first devise a **SELECT** statement which returns the names and student numbers of those students who have received A's. There is one hitch, however: what if a student has received an A in more than one class? If so, the student's name and number will appear more than once in the results of the **SELECT**. Since SQL does not prohibit duplicate records in a table, using this **SELECT** within an **INSERT** will cause more than one record to be added to the **TEACHERS** table for that student. We can avoid this by specifying the **DISTINCT** option on the **SELECT**. Recall that when **DISTINCT** is used, any duplicates which would otherwise appear in the results of the **SELECT** will be eliminated, leaving only one record per student.

A correct formulation of the desired **SELECT** statement is

```
SELECT DISTINCT student#, student_name
    FROM STUDENTS, ENROLLS
    WHERE STUDENTS.student# = ENROLLS.student# AND
            grade = 4;
```

Next, this query must be embedded within the **INSERT**, like

```
INSERT INTO TEACHERS (teacher#, teacher_name)
    SELECT DISTINCT student#, student_name
        FROM STUDENTS, ENROLLS
        WHERE STUDENTS.student# = ENROLLS.student# AND
                grade = 4;
```

When this statement is executed, the **TEACHERS** table will swell to include several new records. Each of those new records will have a **teacher#** equivalent to that student's **student#**, and that student's **student_name** as its **teacher_name**.

The fields **phone** and **salary** in each of those newly added records will be set to **NULL**. As usual, the **SELECT** statement used within the **INSERT** can be as complex as desired. It could contain a subquery or any other legal option within its **WHERE** clause.

An important note: assuming the **TEACHERS** table was created as in the example from the last chapter, the **teacher#** column is constrained to be **UNIQUE**. If the value in **student#** for one of the new records being added were identical to that for an existing **teacher#**, that record would not be added to the table. In the example database, this doesn't happen, but in a similar real world application it might. The restrictions specified when a table is created apply to all records added, no matter what technique is used to add them.

Example: adding records to a table using a SELECT statement

• Problem

Promote all students who received an A in any class to teachers, using their current student number as teacher number.

• Query Diagram

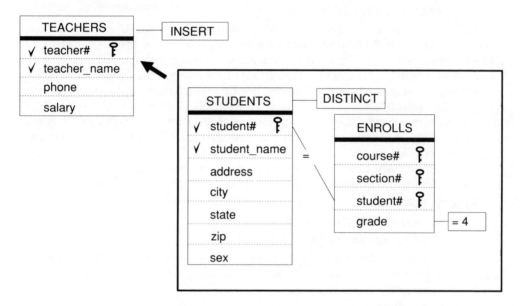

• SQL

```
INSERT INTO TEACHERS (teacher#, teacher_name)
    SELECT DISTINCT student#, student_name
        FROM STUDENTS, ENROLLS
        WHERE  STUDENTS.student# = ENROLLS.student# AND
            grade = 4;
```

Modifying Records in a Table

Once a record is in a table, it may be necessary to modify one or more of its values. This is accomplished with SQL's **UPDATE** statement. The general form of an **UPDATE** is

```
UPDATE <table>
    SET <column name> = <value>
    WHERE <predicate>;
```

The table containing the record or records to be modified is specified in **<table>**. Following the word **SET** appear one or more expressions of the form **<column name>=<value>**. Each of these must first name a column in that table, then specify a new value for that column, either a constant or an expression of some kind. Finally, a **WHERE** clause may optionally appear, limiting which records the modifications apply to. If no **WHERE** clause is used, the changes apply to all records in the specified table. Like many other SQL statements (all except **SELECT**, in fact) **UPDATE** returns no results, with the possible exception of a message indicating successful modification of the specified records.

Suppose, for instance, that we wished to increase Dr. Horn's salary to $28,450.00. This could be accomplished with

```
UPDATE TEACHERS
    SET salary = 28450.00
    WHERE teacher_name = 'Dr. Horn';
```

We can even modify existing values using arithmetic operations. For example, to give Dr. Horn a 5 percent cost of living increase along with a $1,000.00 merit raise, you could type

```
UPDATE TEACHERS
    SET salary = (salary * 1.05) + 1000
    WHERE teacher_name = 'Dr. Horn';
```

This statement starts with Dr. Horn's old salary, increases it by 5 percent, adds 1000, then puts the result back in the **salary** field of Dr. Horn's record. (In this example, the parentheses around **salary * 1.05** aren't really required, since multiplication is by default performed before addition. Using parentheses never hurts, though, and usually makes things clearer to a human reader.)

It is possible to modify more than one column at a time. The columns to be updated, together with their new values, are separated by commas and listed after the word **SET**. For example, to both add Dr. Lowe's first name and change her phone number, one could type

```
UPDATE TEACHERS
    SET phone = '257-3080',
        teacher_name = 'Dr. Carla Lowe'
    WHERE teacher_name = 'Dr. Lowe';
```

Note that the order in which the column names are listed is not significant.

So far, every example has contained a **WHERE** clause. As mentioned earlier, however, the **WHERE** clause is optional in an **UPDATE**. If it is omitted, the update applies to all records in the table. For example, to give *all* teachers a 5 percent cost of living increase and a $1,000.00 merit raise, the command is

```
UPDATE TEACHERS
     SET salary = (salary * 1.05) + 1000;
```

Because no **WHERE** clause is specified to limit the records affected, this **UPDATE** modifies the **salary** field of every record in the **TEACHERS** table.

If a **WHERE** clause is used, it can be as complex as desired. For instance, suppose we wish to give a 7.5 percent raise to all teachers earning less than the average salary. To determine the average salary, it is easiest to use SQL's **AVG** function. Because aggregates such as **AVG** cannot be used directly in a **WHERE** clause, however, we must specify an appropriate subquery, like

```
UPDATE TEACHERS
     SET salary = salary * 1.075
     WHERE salary <
          (SELECT AVG(salary)
           FROM TEACHERS);
```

This statement will modify the salary fields of only those records in **TEACHERS** whose salary is below the average. (Note that the average salary will be calculated only once, before any records are changed. If it were recalculated after each change, the average would itself change, leading to peculiar results.)

Example: updating a record

• Problem

Increase Dr. Horn's salary to $28,450.00.

• Query Diagram

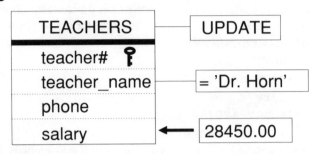

• SQL

```
UPDATE TEACHERS
    SET salary = 28450.00
    WHERE teacher_name = 'Dr. Horn';
```

• Results

teacher#	teacher_name	phone	salary
303	Dr. Horn	257-3049	28450.00

• Note

UPDATE typically returns no results. These examples include results only to help clarify the effect of the **UPDATE** statement.

Example: updating a record using arithmetic operations

• *Problem*

Give Dr. Horn a 5 percent cost of living increase and a $1,000 merit raise.

• *Query Diagram*

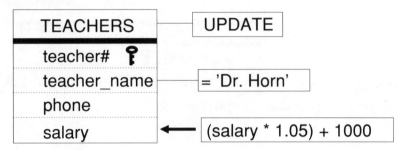

• *SQL*

```
UPDATE TEACHERS
    SET salary = (salary * 1.05) + 1000
    WHERE teacher_name = 'Dr. Horn';
```

• *Results*

teacher#	teacher_name	phone	salary
303	Dr. Horn	257-3049	29917.00

Example: updating more than one field in a record at once

• Problem

Change Dr. Lowe's phone number, and add her first name.

• Query Diagram

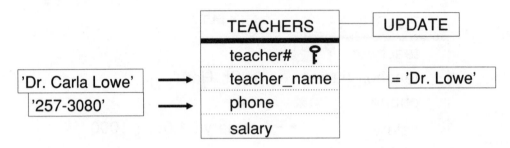

• SQL

```
UPDATE TEACHERS
    SET phone = '257-3080',
        teacher_name = 'Dr. Carla Lowe'
    WHERE teacher_name = 'Dr. Lowe';
```

• Results

teacher#	teacher_name	phone	salary
290	Dr. Carla Lowe	257-3080	31450.00

Example: updating several records using arithmetic operations

• Problem

Give all teachers a 5 percent cost of living increase and a $1,000 merit raise.

• Query Diagram

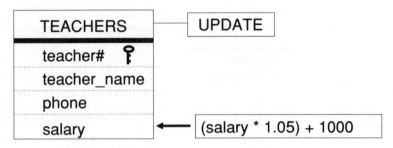

• SQL

```
UPDATE TEACHERS
    SET salary = (salary * 1.05) + 1000;
```

• Results

teacher#	teacher_name	phone	salary
303	Dr. Horn	257-3049	29917.00
290	Dr. Lowe	257-2390	34022.50
430	Dr. Engle	256-4621	41110.00
180	Dr. Cooke	257-8088	32038.00
560	Dr. Olsen	257-8086	34366.90
784	Dr. Scango	257-3046	34702.90

Example: updating a record using a subquery

• *Problem*

Give all teachers whose salary is below average a 7.5 percent raise.

• *Query Diagram*

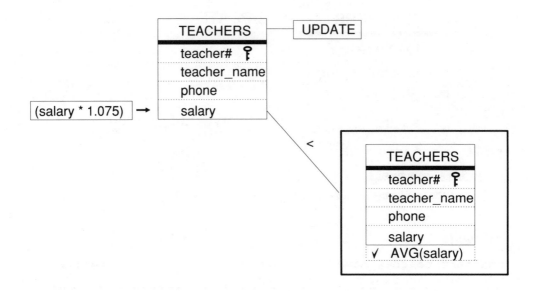

• *SQL*

```
UPDATE TEACHERS
    SET salary = salary * 1.075
    WHERE salary <
         (SELECT AVG(salary)
              FROM TEACHERS);
```

• *Results*

teacher#	teacher_name	phone	salary
303	Dr. Horn	257-3049	30105.50
290	Dr. Lowe	257-2390	34308.75
180	Dr. Cooke	257-8088	32277.00

Deleting Records From a Table

Deleting one or several records from a table is very straightforward. The general form of the statement used, **DELETE**, is

DELETE FROM <table>

    WHERE <predicate>;

When this statement is used, **<table>** is replaced by the name of the table from which the records are to be deleted. All records for which the **<predicate>** is true will be deleted. (As will be described shortly, the **WHERE** clause can sometimes be omitted.) In some ways, **DELETE** is similar to **SELECT**. Instead of simply returning the selected records, however, **DELETE** removes them from the table.

A **DELETE** may remove one or several records, depending on what is specified in the **WHERE** clause. For instance, if student number 210 flunks out, his record can be removed with

DELETE FROM STUDENTS

    WHERE student# = 210;

In fact, the **WHERE** clause can be just as complex as a **WHERE** clause in a **SELECT**, allowing a great deal of flexibility in identifying the records to be deleted.

SQL also provides a very easy way to delete all records from a table: simply omit the **WHERE** clause. If, for example, we wished to delete the record of every student, we could type

DELETE FROM STUDENTS;

while to delete all the **TEACHERS** records, the command is

DELETE FROM TEACHERS;

Example: deleting a record from a table

• Problem

Delete all records in the **ENROLLS** table which contain **NULL** grades.

• Query Diagram

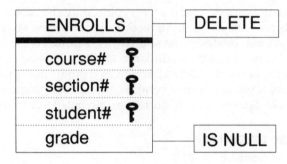

• SQL

```
DELETE FROM ENROLLS
    WHERE grade IS NULL;
```

Example: deleting a record from a table

• *Problem*

Delete every record in the **ENROLLS** table that has no matching record in the **STUDENTS** table.

• *Query Diagram*

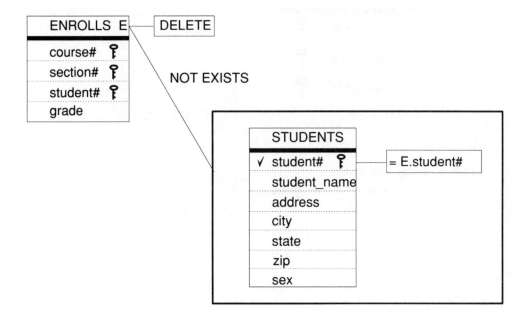

• *SQL*

```
DELETE FROM ENROLLS E
    WHERE NOT EXISTS
        (SELECT student#
            FROM STUDENTS
            WHERE STUDENTS.student# = E.student#);
```

• *Note*

Ideally, no records should exist in **ENROLLS** that don't have matching records in **STUDENTS**. In real databases, however, it is not uncommon for records to be added erroneously. Many relational DBMS's provide only limited support for what is called *referential integrity*, ensuring that the information stored in a database is internally consistent. Instead, the responsibility for ensuring this integrity rests with the users of the database.

Example: deleting several records from a table

• Problem

Remove all records containing invalid grades from the **ENROLLS** table.

• Query Diagram

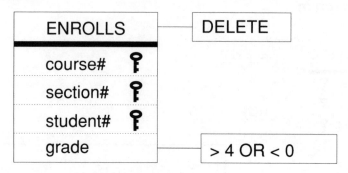

• SQL

```
DELETE FROM ENROLLS
    WHERE grade > 4 or grade < 0;
```

Example: deleting all records from a table

• Problem

Remove all records from the **ENROLLS** table.

• Query Diagram

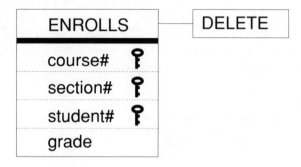

• SQL

```
DELETE FROM ENROLLS;
```

Views

9

The tables that make up a relational database have a physical existence—the data stored in them actually takes up space in some computer system. Based on these actual physical tables, however, we can define other tables which have no physical existence, but nevertheless can be accessed as if they did. Such tables are called *views*.

Creating Views

A view is a table created from all or part of one or more existing tables. Because of their lack of physical existence, views are sometimes called *virtual tables*, while the tables which physically exist in the database are called *real* or, more commonly, *base tables*. To emphasize this distinction, views are represented in query diagrams using dashed lines.

Like tables, views are created with the **CREATE** statement. Unlike tables, the rows and columns comprising a view must already exist in one or more tables (or views) in the database.

The general form of a SQL statement which creates a view is

```
CREATE VIEW <view> (<column names>) AS
    SELECT <column names>
        FROM <table>
        WHERE <predicate>;
```

As with table creation, the words **CREATE VIEW** inform SQL of our intentions, and **<view>** is the name assigned to the newly created view. Because a view is just a table (like everything else in a relational database), its columns may be named by specifying a parenthesized list of names in **<column names>**. This is optional, however; if this parenthesized list is omitted, the names of the view's columns will be those of the **<column names>** specified in the defining **SELECT** statement.

This **SELECT** statement can be as complex as necessary. It may perform a join with two or more tables, include a subquery, or even use **GROUP BY**. In any case, the table which results from the **SELECT** *is* the view.

Creating Views Based On One Table

The simplest views draw their records from only a single base table. In fact, one common reason to use views is to limit access to the information stored in a table. Suppose, for example, that we wished to allow students access to the example database, but did not want them to be able to see teachers' salaries. To allow this, we could create a view called **FACULTY** which includes everything from **TEACHERS** except the salary column. This view could be created with

```
CREATE VIEW FACULTY AS
    SELECT teacher#, teacher_name, phone
        FROM TEACHERS;
```

Because no new column names were specified, the column names of the view **FACULTY** are inherited from the selected columns in **TEACHERS**: **teacher#**, **teacher_name**, and **phone**. In general, this view functions just as if it were a base table: a user could, for instance, use a **SELECT** statement referencing this view to learn a particular teacher's phone number. But since it does not include the column called **salary** from **TEACHERS**, accessors of this view could not retrieve that information. Students, therefore, could be allowed to access this view to retrieve information about their instructors, but access to the actual **TEACHERS** table, and thus to salary information, would be restricted only to university administrators. (SQL's tools for granting and revoking access to tables are described in the next chapter.)

Another simple example: we may frequently wish to access the names and student numbers of students from Pennsylvania. To facilitate easy access to this information, we could define a view called **PA_ONLY** with

```
CREATE VIEW PA_ONLY (name, number, state) AS
    SELECT student_name, student#, state
        FROM STUDENTS
        WHERE state = 'PA';
```

In this example, we have changed the name and order of the columns in the view from those found in the base table **STUDENTS**. This view will contain only the specified columns from those records in **STUDENTS** which satisfy the **WHERE** clause given, i.e., the names, student numbers, and states of all students from Pennsylvania.

It is even possible to create views which include columns not present in any base table, but which are instead derived from base table information. Such columns are sometimes called *derived columns*. If, for instance, we were frequently interested in seeing the teachers' monthly salaries, we might define a view like

```
CREATE VIEW MONTHLY (teacher_name, teacher#, m_salary) AS
    SELECT teacher_name, teacher#, salary / 12
        FROM TEACHERS;
```

The resulting view contains a derived column of monthly salary values, information not directly found in any base table. For use with later **SELECT**s, however, the view **MONTHLY** can be used just like any other table.

Example: creating a view

• *Problem*

Create a view including all columns from the **TEACHERS** table except salary.

• *Query Diagram*

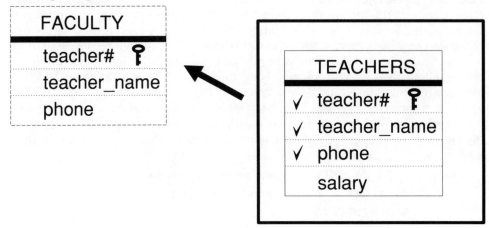

• *SQL*

```
CREATE VIEW FACULTY AS
    SELECT teacher#, teacher_name, phone
        FROM TEACHERS;
```

Example: creating a view

• Problem

Create a view containing only the records from **STUDENTS** for students from Pennsylvania.

• Query Diagram

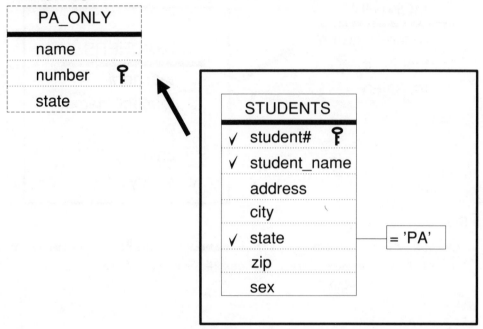

• SQL

```
CREATE VIEW PA_ONLY (name, number, state) AS
   SELECT student_name, student#, state
      FROM STUDENTS
      WHERE state = 'PA';
```

Example: creating a view with a derived column

• Problem

Create a view containing each teacher's name, number, and monthly salary.

• Query Diagram

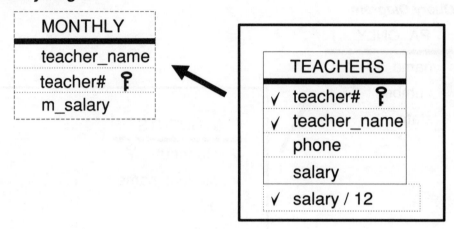

• SQL

```
CREATE VIEW MONTHLY (teacher_name, teacher#, m_salary) AS
    SELECT teacher_name, teacher#, salary / 12
        FROM TEACHERS;
```

Creating Views Based On More Than One Table

Views need not draw their records from just one table. Since a view can be defined which consists of the records resulting from any **SELECT** statement, the view may draw its values from two or more tables. Although slightly more complex to create, such views can be very useful.

Suppose, for example, that we often wished to refer to a summary of course information which included each course's name, its course number, and the number of students in each section. To make our lives easier, we could define a view that contained exactly this information. Since this information is contained in two different tables, however, the view must be based on a join, like

```
CREATE VIEW SUMMARY AS
    SELECT course_name, C.course#, section#,
           num_students
        FROM COURSES C, SECTIONS S
        WHERE S.course# = C.course#;
```

Once again, the column names of the view are inherited from those in the base tables **SECTIONS** and **COURSES**. The contents of the view are those records which result from this **CREATE VIEW**'s join. (As usual, the aliases **S** and **C** are simply a convenience; they aren't a required part of view definitions.)

Views can be based on as many tables as desired. For instance, to create a roster for all courses, listing for each its teacher, course name, and the names and grades of all its students, one could type

```
CREATE VIEW ROSTER AS
    SELECT teacher_name, course_name,
           student_name, grade
        FROM TEACHERS, COURSES, SECTIONS,
           ENROLLS, STUDENTS
        WHERE TEACHERS.teacher# = SECTIONS.teacher# AND
              SECTIONS.section# = ENROLLS.section# AND
              SECTIONS.course# = ENROLLS.course# AND
              COURSES.course# = SECTIONS.course# AND
              ENROLLS.student# = STUDENTS.student#;
```

Both this and the previously defined view can be used like any other table in **SELECT** statements.

Example: creating a view using a join with two tables

• Problem

Create a view containing the name, number, and enrollment for each section of each course.

• Query Diagram

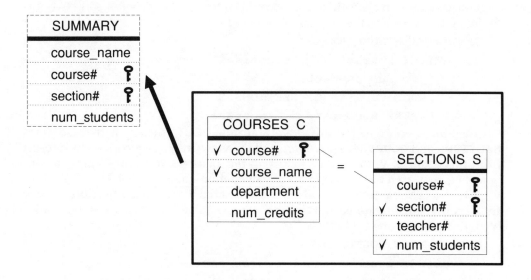

• SQL

```
CREATE VIEW SUMMARY AS
    SELECT course_name, C.course#,
            section#, num_students
        FROM COURSES C, SECTIONS S
        WHERE S.course# = C.course#;
```

Example: creating a view using a join with five tables

• *Problem*

Create a view containing the roster of each class, including students' grades.

• *Query Diagram*

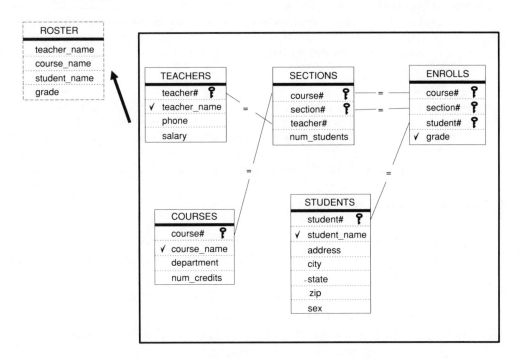

• *SQL*

```
CREATE VIEW ROSTER AS
    SELECT teacher_name, course_name,
           student_name, grade
       FROM TEACHERS, SECTIONS, ENROLLS
           COURSES, STUDENTS
       WHERE TEACHERS.teacher# = SECTIONS.teacher# AND
           SECTIONS.section# = ENROLLS.section# AND
           SECTIONS.course# = ENROLLS.course# AND
           COURSES.course# = SECTIONS.course# AND
           ENROLLS.student# = STUDENTS.student#;
```

Queries Using Views

In some types of queries, views act identically to base tables. In others, particularly those which add, modify, or delete records, views have some restrictions and can't support certain operations which are perfectly legal on base tables.

Selecting Records from a View

As stated earlier, information can be retrieved from views just as if they were base tables. Queries with **SELECT**, then, operate normally on views. For example, to list all records in the view **FACULTY**, one could type

```
SELECT *
    FROM FACULTY;
```

The result is a list of exactly what the **CREATE VIEW** statement defined to be in this view: names, teacher numbers, and phone numbers of all teachers.

SELECTs operating on views can also have **WHERE** clauses, and, in general, are allowed to be as complex as those operating on base tables. For example, to retrieve the names and grades of only those students in Dr. Engle's class from the view **ROSTER**, you could type

```
SELECT student_name, grade
    FROM ROSTER
    WHERE teacher_name = 'Dr. Engle';
```

This same information could be retrieved from the base tables themselves with

```
SELECT student_name, grade
    FROM STUDENTS, TEACHERS, ENROLLS, SECTIONS
    WHERE teacher_name = 'Dr. Engle' AND
            TEACHERS.teacher# = SECTIONS.teacher# AND
            SECTIONS.course# = ENROLLS.course# AND
            SECTIONS.section# = ENROLLS.section# AND
            ENROLLS.student# = STUDENTS.student#;
```

Clearly, the query using the view **ROSTER** is much simpler. If this kind of information will be requested often, defining an appropriate view will make life much simpler.

Nothing is free, however, not even with SQL. A reasonable question to ask is, if a view has no physical existence, how can SQL correctly carry out queries against it? The answer stems from how SQL actually stores a view. Typically, a SQL implementation will store the **SELECT** statement you used in the **CREATE VIEW** statement. Then, whenever a query attempts to access that view, SQL must first (conceptually) execute the **SELECT** which defines the view, then execute that new query. The predictable result is that, while views provide convenience and some measure of security, they do so at the cost of efficiency. As a result, queries accessing views are likely to execute more slowly than those accessing only base tables.

Example: listing all records in a view

• Problem

List all records in the view **FACULTY**.

• Query Diagram

```
┌─────────────────────────┐
│       FACULTY           │
├─────────────────────────┤
│  √  teacher#  ?         │
│  √  teacher_name        │
│  √  phone               │
└─────────────────────────┘
```

• SQL

```
SELECT *
    FROM FACULTY;
```

• Results

```
teacher# teacher_name        phone

     303 Dr. Horn            257-3049
     290 Dr. Lowe            257-2390
     430 Dr. Engle           256-4621
     180 Dr. Cooke           257-8088
     560 Dr. Olsen           257-8086
     784 Dr. Scango          257-3046
```

Example: listing all records in a view

• *Problem*

List all records in the view **PA_ONLY**.

• *Query Diagram*

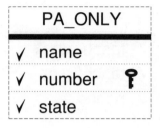

• *SQL*

```
SELECT *
    FROM PA_ONLY;
```

• *Results*

name	number	state
Susan Powell	148	PA
Janet Ladd	354	PA
Janet Thomas	654	PA

Example: listing only some of a view's records

• Problem

From the view **ROSTER**, list the names and grades of students in Dr. Engle's class.

• Query Diagram

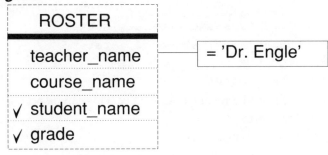

• SQL

```
SELECT student_name, grade
    FROM ROSTER
    WHERE teacher_name = 'Dr. Engle';
```

• Results

student_name	grade
Howard Mansfield	3
Joe Adams	4
Allen Thomas	2

Adding Records to a View

Updating a view—adding, modifying, or deleting its records—can be problematic. Because views are dependent on base tables and have no physical existence on their own, it is not always possible to correctly update a view. In an academic sense, updating views remains an interesting research topic. From a more pragmatic perspective, updating views can be a headache.

Consider the view **PA_ONLY**, defined earlier, consisting of the names, student numbers, and states of only those students from Pennsylvania. It was created with

```
CREATE VIEW PA_ONLY (name, number, state) AS
    SELECT student_name, student#, state
        FROM STUDENTS
        WHERE state = 'PA';
```

Suppose we want to add a record to this view. This can be accomplished with

```
INSERT INTO PA_ONLY
    VALUES ('Patti Couture',
            335,
            'PA');
```

How is this statement handled by SQL? Because this view relies on only a single base table, the answer is straightforward: by adding a record to the **STUDENTS** table. That record will contain the value 'Patti Couture' in its **student_name** field, 335 in **student#**, and 'PA' in **state**. All other fields in this new record—**address**, **city**, **zip**, and **sex**—will be set to **NULL**.

What happens if an attempt is made to insert a record which does not conform to the requirements specified in the **CREATE VIEW** statement? One might, for example, type

```
INSERT INTO PA_ONLY
    VALUES ('Kay Gensmer',
            442
            'MN');
```

Because its value for **state** is 'MN', this new record violates the condition given in the **WHERE** clause when the view **PA_ONLY** was created. What will SQL do in this case? Should it insert the new (but in some sense illegal) record into **STUDENTS**, or should it reject this **INSERT** statement?

The answer depends on how the view was created. According to the SQL standard, a view can be created with the **CHECK** option. Although not all systems implement it, this option requires SQL to check view updates for consistency with the original view definition, and to reject any that violate the view's constraints. To create **PA_ONLY** with this option, one types

```
CREATE VIEW PA_ONLY (name, number, state) AS
    SELECT student_name, student#, state
        FROM STUDENTS
        WHERE state = 'PA'
    WITH CHECK OPTION;
```

If the view were created this way, the above attempt to **INSERT** a record with **state** equal to 'MN' would have been rejected. If the **CHECK** option were not specified during creation of the view, the erroneous record would have been added to the **STUDENTS** table but would not have been visible in the view **PA_ONLY**. (It's interesting to note that while views have this sort of automatic checking mechanism defined for them, the SQL standard includes no similar mechanism for base tables.)

Even worse problems can occur with views which include derived columns. Consider the view **MONTHLY**, defined earlier as

```
CREATE VIEW MONTHLY (teacher_name, teacher#, m_salary) AS
    SELECT teacher_name, teacher#, salary / 12
        FROM TEACHERS;
```

Suppose we now attempt to add a new record to this view with

```
INSERT INTO MONTHLY
    VALUES ('Jeanne Fennell',
        544
        2995.00);
```

While our **INSERT** statement is perfectly correct, there is no way for SQL to correctly execute it. To see why, try to answer this question: what base table should this new record be added to? The **TEACHERS** table, on which the view **MONTHLY** is based, has no column containing monthly salary, and thus no place to store the value 2995.00 from the new record. While it might be argued that SQL should understand that 2995.00 is one-twelfth of a value which could be stored in **salary**, and thus calculate the appropriate amount to store in that column in **TEACHERS**, this is not done in practice. The upshot is quite simple: updates such as this will be rejected as illegal by SQL.

One other point: all the updates discussed so far involve views based only on a single table. With views such as **ROSTER**, dependent on many tables, adding records again becomes a problem. In general, views based on more than one table are not updatable. Also, even though views can be defined using **SELECT** statements with **GROUP BY** and **HAVING** clauses, such views are also not updatable.

Example: adding a record to a view

• Problem

Add a new record for Patti Couture, student number 335, to the view **PA_ONLY**.

• Query Diagram

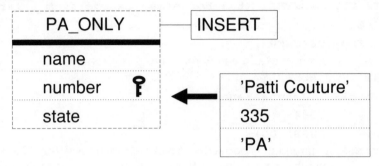

• SQL

```
INSERT INTO PA_ONLY
    VALUES ('Patti Couture',
            335,
            'PA');
```

Modifying Records in a View

Similar difficulties arise with attempts to modify records in views. Some views, such as **PA_ONLY** above, can be modified with statements like

```
UPDATE PA_ONLY
    SET name = 'Kenneth Myrvold'
    WHERE number = 654;
```

In this case, the appropriate record in **STUDENTS**, the view's base table, is modified. But suppose the **UPDATE** had looked like

```
UPDATE PA_ONLY
    SET name = 'Kenneth Myrvold',
        state = 'CA'
    WHERE number = 654;
```

Again, we are faced with a possible inconsistency, since the requested modifications would cause this record to no longer meet the requirements for membership in this view. Whether such an **UPDATE** is accepted or rejected by SQL depends again on whether the **CHECK** option was specified when the view was created.

Modifying records in views with derived columns, such as **MONTHLY** above, may be allowed as long as no attempt is made to change a value in a derived column. Recall that all queries on views, whether simple **SELECTS** or more invasive **INSERT**s and **UPDATE**s, must eventually be converted into SQL operations on the view's base tables. If this is not possible, as in the case of updating a value in a derived column, the query against the view must be rejected.

Example: modifying a record in a view

• Problem

Change the name of the student whose number is 654 to Kenneth Myrvold in the view **PA_ONLY**.

• Query Diagram

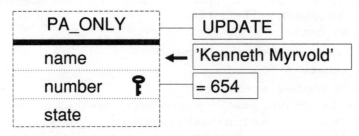

• SQL

```
UPDATE PA_ONLY
    SET name = 'Kenneth Myrvold'
    WHERE number = 654;
```

Deleting Records From a View

With this understanding in mind, it is no great leap to predict how SQL's **DELETE** statement will work with views. If possible, records will be deleted from the base table to cause the desired effect in the view. For example, the statement

```
DELETE FROM PA_ONLY
    WHERE number = 335;
```

will remove the record with the value **335** in its **student#** field from **STUDENTS**. In turn, that record would vanish from the view **PA_ONLY**. (Note that *all* of the record's fields are deleted, not just those included in the view.) There are times, however, when this will not be possible. In such situations, SQL must reject the attempted deletion.

In general, when is a view updatable? When can **INSERT**s, **UPDATE**s, and **DELETE**s safely be executed against a view? The answer depends to some extent on choices made by the implementors of your particular system. It is safe to say, however, that a view is probably *not* updatable if it relies on more than one base table, or if its defining **SELECT** uses **DISTINCT** or includes a **GROUP BY** clause, a **HAVING** clause, or a subquery. Also, views with one or more derived columns will have at least some restrictions on their updatability.

Example: deleting a record from a view

• *Problem*

Delete the student whose number is 335 from the view **PA_ONLY**.

• *Query Diagram*

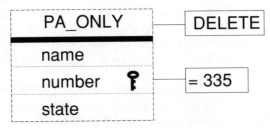

• *SQL*

```
DELETE FROM PA_ONLY
    WHERE number = 335;
```

Destroying (Dropping) Views

Views are destroyed in the same way as are tables: via SQL's **DROP** statement. The general form of a statement for destroying a view is

```
DROP VIEW <view>;
```

This is just like destroying tables, except for the use of the word **VIEW** in place of **TABLE**. As with table deletion, the name of the view to be dropped is substituted for **<view>**.

To drop the view **FACULTY**, for example, the command is

```
DROP VIEW FACULTY;
```

while to drop **ROSTER** you would type

```
DROP VIEW ROSTER;
```

The number of base tables used to create the view makes no difference; every view is dropped using a single **DROP VIEW** statement.

Example: destroying (dropping) a view

• Problem

Drop the view **FACULTY**.

• Query Diagram

• SQL

```
DROP VIEW FACULTY;
```

Example: destroying (dropping) a view

• *Problem*

Drop the view **ROSTER**.

• *Query Diagram*

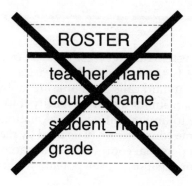

• *SQL*

```
DROP VIEW ROSTER;
```

Granting and Revoking Privileges

10

Most relational database systems allow access to their stored data by more than one user. Each of those users is typically required to give their user name before accessing the system. The SQL standard calls this name an "authorization identifier" but defines no standard mechanism for a user to specify it to the database system; instead, each system is free to implement its own. Relational systems such as DB2, running on large mainframe computers, can be used by many people at once, while others, like those used on personal computers, allow access by only one person at a time. In either case, more than one user potentially has access to the system's tables.

This can be a problem. While SQL's primary purpose of allowing access to stored data is an important function, there are some situations in which *preventing* access is more important. To allow its users to control who can read and modify their tables, SQL includes statements allowing its users to grant and revoke various *privileges*. Via these statements, a user can control exactly who is allowed access to which tables.

Granting Privileges

When you create a table using SQL's **CREATE** statement, that table belongs to you. To keep track of this, SQL will internally precede the table's name with your user name. For instance, if the **TEACHERS** table had actually been created by Dr. Engle with

```
CREATE TABLE TEACHERS
    (teacher# SMALLINT,
    teacher_name CHAR (18),
    phone CHAR (10),
    salary FLOAT);
```

SQL would have internally named this table **ENGLE.TEACHERS** (assuming Dr. Engle's user name was **ENGLE**).

This fact implies the answer to another important question: what happens if two different users create tables with the same name? SQL resolves this problem by internally preceding the name of each with the user name of its creator. To access a table created by another user, then, you may be required to specify its full name, such as **ENGLE.TEACHERS**. For your own tables, SQL knows who you are (remember, you specified your user name before accessing the database), so it automatically precedes references to your tables with the appropriate name—yours.

The creator of a table is its owner, and can read, modify, and add records to or delete records from it. The rights to perform these various operations are defined by SQL as different privileges. The privileges which a user has for a particular table limit the access he or she has to that table. The available privileges are:

- **SELECT**: allows **SELECT** statements to be executed on the table;
- **INSERT**: allows the addition of new records to the table with **INSERT** statements;
- **DELETE**: allows existing records in the table to be removed with **DELETE** statements;
- **UPDATE**: allows records in the table to be modified with **UPDATE** statements.

When a table is created, its creator possesses all of these privileges. No other user has any of them. No one but its creator, therefore, may access this new table in any way. Before any other user can do anything with the table, its owner must assign that user one or more of the above privileges. This is accomplished via SQL's **GRANT** statement.

The general form of **GRANT** is

```
GRANT <privileges> ON <table> TO <user>;
```

where **<privileges>** indicates which privileges are to be granted, **<table>** is the name of the table concerned, and **<user>** is the user name of the user to whom the privileges are being granted. For example, if after its creation Dr. Engle wanted to allow Dr. Horn to read the information stored in **TEACHERS**, he would type

```
GRANT SELECT ON TEACHERS TO HORN;
```

It is also possible to grant several privileges at once, like

```
GRANT SELECT, UPDATE, INSERT ON TEACHERS TO HORN;
```

Dr. Horn is now allowed to read and modify records stored in **TEACHERS**, as well as add new ones. It is even possible to grant all privileges at once, using the shorthand **ALL PRIVILEGES**, like

```
GRANT ALL PRIVILEGES ON TEACHERS TO HORN;
```

The word **PRIVILEGES** is optional, so

```
GRANT ALL ON TEACHERS TO HORN;
```

has the same effect. Dr. Horn can now perform any legal SQL operations on the **TEACHERS** table.

Permissions can also be granted to several users at once. If Dr. Engle wanted to allow both Dr. Lowe and Dr. Olsen to read **TEACHERS**, he could type

```
GRANT SELECT ON TEACHERS TO LOWE, OLSEN;
```

To grant one or more privileges to all users of a database, the word **PUBLIC** can be used, like

```
GRANT SELECT ON TEACHERS TO PUBLIC;
```

It is even possible to grant all privileges on a table to all users via

```
GRANT ALL ON TEACHERS TO PUBLIC;
```

In some cases, the owner of a table may want others to have access only to part of a table. To allow this, the **GRANT** statement allows privileges to be granted on specific columns only. It is reasonable, for instance, to expect that information about teacher salaries not be generally available, while the other information in the **TEACHERS** table can be read by anyone. The owner of **TEACHERS** could allow just this sort of access with

```
GRANT SELECT(teacher#, teacher_name, phone) ON TEACHERS
     TO PUBLIC;
```
(The SQL standard only allows column names to be specified with the **UPDATE** privilege, while all other privileges must allow access to every column in a table. Some implementations of SQL, however, allow specific columns to be identified for other privileges, as well.)

Granting Privileges On Views

Views, created with SQL's **CREATE VIEW** statement, also have privileges. For the most part, granting these privileges is just like granting privileges on tables. For example, to allow Dr. Horn to read the information in the view **FACULTY**, its owner would type

```
GRANT SELECT ON FACULTY TO HORN;
```
while to allow that same access to all users, he or she would type

```
GRANT SELECT ON FACULTY TO PUBLIC;
```

Life gets more complex, however, when granting **INSERT**, **DELETE**, or **UPDATE** privileges on a view. Recall that a view may or may not be updatable, depending on how it is defined. For some views, new records cannot be added or deleted, nor can all fields in existing records be modified. As described in the last chapter, these restrictions are intrinsic in the definition of the view. For these types of views, not all privileges may be granted, since the operations that those permissions would allow are illegal.

Example: granting read privileges to a specific user

• Problem

Allow Dr. Horn to read the **TEACHERS** table.

• Query Diagram

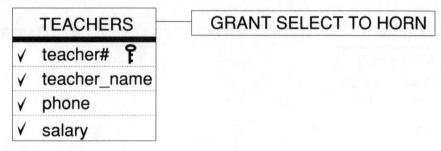

• SQL

```
GRANT SELECT ON TEACHERS TO HORN;
```

Example: granting several privileges at once to a specific user

• Problem

Allow Dr. Horn to read, modify, and add to the **TEACHERS** table.

• Query Diagram

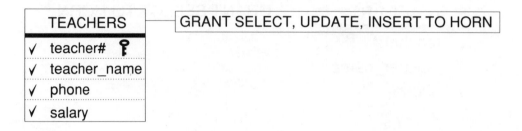

• SQL

```
GRANT SELECT, UPDATE,  INSERT ON TEACHERS TO HORN;
```

Example: granting all privileges to a specific user

• Problem

Allow Dr. Horn complete access to the **TEACHERS** table.

• Query Diagram

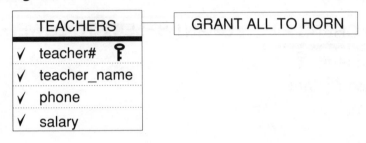

• SQL

```
GRANT ALL ON TEACHERS TO HORN;
```

Example: granting privileges to more than one user

• Problem

Allow both Dr. Lowe and Dr. Olsen to read the **TEACHERS** table.

• Query Diagram

TEACHERS	GRANT SELECT TO LOWE, OLSEN
✓ teacher# ♀	
✓ teacher_name	
✓ phone	
✓ salary	

• SQL

```
GRANT SELECT ON TEACHERS TO LOWE, OLSEN;
```

Example: granting privileges to all users

• Problem

Allow all users to read the **TEACHERS** table.

• Query Diagram

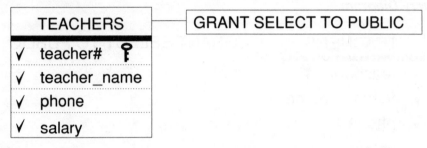

• SQL

```
GRANT SELECT ON TEACHERS TO PUBLIC;
```

Example: granting read privileges on specific columns in a table to all users

• Problem

Allow anyone to read all but the salary information in the **TEACHERS** table.

• Query Diagram

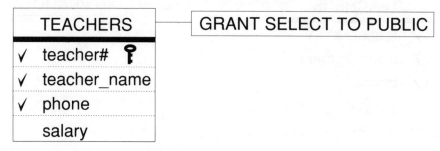

• SQL

```
GRANT SELECT(teacher#, teacher_name, phone) ON TEACHERS
    TO PUBLIC;
```

Example: granting read privileges on a view to all users

• Problem

Allow anyone to read the view **FACULTY**.

• Query Diagram

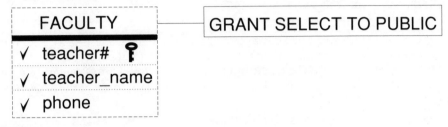

• SQL

```
GRANT SELECT ON FACULTY TO PUBLIC;
```

Passing Privileges On: The GRANT Option

SQL also allows granting privileges to a user, then allowing that user to grant those privileges to others. For this, the language provides the **GRANT** option. For example, its owner could allow Dr. Lowe complete access to the **ENROLLS** table *and* give her the right to grant complete or partial access to **ENROLLS** to any other user with

```
GRANT ALL ON ENROLLS TO LOWE
     WITH GRANT OPTION;
```

The phrase **WITH GRANT OPTION**, appearing at the end of the **GRANT** statement, means that the right to grant privileges is passed on to Dr. Lowe.

Similarly, the owner of the **COURSES** table could allow Drs. Olsen and Engle to read and modify its records, as well as passing on the right to grant these privileges with

```
GRANT SELECT, UPDATE ON COURSES TO OLSEN, ENGLE
     WITH GRANT OPTION;
```

Drs. Olsen and Engle may now themselves read and update **COURSES**, and they may also grant other users the right to read and update **COURSES**. They may not, however, either themselves delete records from, or grant to others the right to delete records from, the **COURSES** table (unless, of course, this right has been granted via some other **GRANT** statement).

As before, **PUBLIC** can be used as a shorthand way to reference all users. In most cases, however, it is not desirable to grant permissions to **PUBLIC** with the **GRANT** option.

Example: granting all privileges to a specific user with the GRANT *option*

• Problem

Allow the user Lowe all permissions on the **ENROLLS** table, and allow her to grant any or all of those permissions to other users.

• Query Diagram

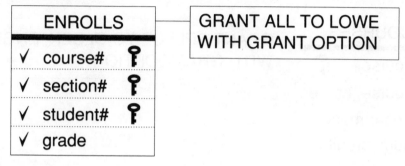

• SQL

```
GRANT ALL ON ENROLLS TO LOWE
     WITH GRANT OPTION;
```

Example: granting read privileges to several users with the GRANT *option*

• Problem

Allow the users Olsen and Engle to read the courses table, and allow them to grant that permission to other users.

• Query Diagram

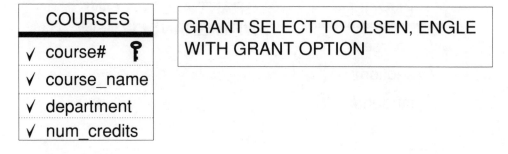

• SQL

```
GRANT SELECT ON COURSES TO OLSEN, ENGLE
    WITH GRANT OPTION;
```

Revoking Privileges

Just as privileges can be granted, they can also be revoked. Another of the idiosyncracies of the SQL standard is its failure to include a mechanism for revoking privileges. Most implementations of SQL, however, perform this essential function with a **REVOKE** statement.

REVOKE operates much like **GRANT**. Just as specific privileges can be granted to specific users, so can specific privileges be revoked from those users. And again, the words **ALL** and **PUBLIC** can be used as shorthand for referring to all privileges and all users, respectively.

For example, to revoke Dr. Horn's update privileges on the **ENROLLS** table, one could type

REVOKE UPDATE ON ENROLLS FROM HORN;

while to revoke insert and delete privileges on the **COURSES** table from Dr. Lowe, the SQL statement is

REVOKE INSERT, DELETE ON COURSES FROM LOWE;

To totally ban Dr. Lowe from accessing the **ENROLLS** table, one would type

REVOKE ALL ON ENROLLS FROM LOWE;

To prevent any users from adding records to, deleting records from, or modifying records in the **STUDENTS** table, you could type

REVOKE INSERT, DELETE, UPDATE ON COURSES
    FROM PUBLIC;

while to allow no access at all to **STUDENTS** by any user other than its owner, the command is

REVOKE ALL ON STUDENTS FROM PUBLIC;

Example: revoking update privileges from a specific user

• Problem

Remove update privileges on the **ENROLLS** table from the user Horn.

• Query Diagram

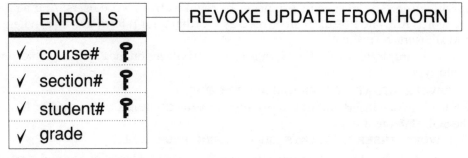

• SQL

```
REVOKE UPDATE ON ENROLLS FROM HORN;
```

Example: revoking all privileges from a specific user

• Problem

Remove all access to the **ENROLLS** table from Dr. Horn.

• Query Diagram

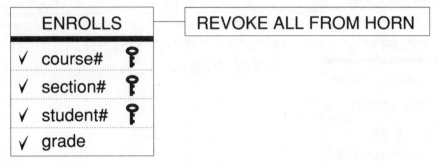

• SQL

```
REVOKE ALL ON ENROLLS FROM HORN;
```

Example: revoking insert and delete privileges from all users

• Problem

Remove insert, delete, and update privileges on the **COURSES** table from all users.

• Query Diagram

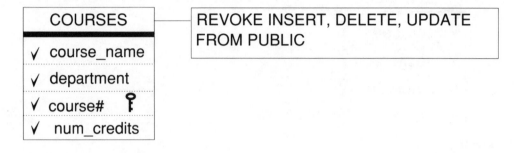

• SQL

```
REVOKE INSERT, DELETE, UPDATE ON COURSES
     FROM PUBLIC;
```

Example: revoking all privileges from all users

• *Problem*

Remove all access to the **STUDENTS** table from all users.

• *Query Diagram*

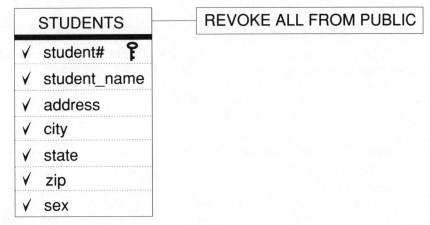

• *SQL*

```
REVOKE ALL ON STUDENTS FROM PUBLIC;
```

Advanced Topics

11

SQL is a powerful tool. The **SELECT** statement, the heart of the language, allows retrieval of information in many different ways, all aimed at answering particular questions. The examples seen so far in no way exhaust what can be done with SQL. In this final chapter, we look at several other ways to use **SELECT** beyond those discussed so far. While you may make only rare use of some of these features, others may find their way into your commonly used SQL subset.

Indexes

Recall that the records stored in a table are unordered. When a new record is added with **INSERT**, SQL simply adds that record in some convenient place in the table. While this lack of order makes for a very simple model of how data is stored, it does not help very much in the efficient retrieval of information. Suppose, for example, that you type

```
SELECT teacher#
    FROM TEACHERS
    WHERE teacher_name = 'Dr. Cooke';
```
To execute this query, SQL must search the entire **TEACHERS** table, comparing the value in each record's **teacher_name** field to 'Dr. Cooke'. When a record is found whose **teacher_name** field contains this value, the value stored in that record's **teacher#** field is returned.

In a small table like **TEACHERS**, performing a simple search like this is unlikely to be a problem. Computers are fast machines, so examining half a dozen records does not take long. In a real relational database, however, a single table may well contain thousands or even millions of records. To try to find Dr. Cooke's teacher number by looking at each record could take a very long time, even with a fast machine. To help solve this problem, SQL allows us to create *indexes*.

An index is simply another table in the database. It cannot, however, be directly queried. Instead, an index is automatically used by SQL itself whenever possible to speed up the execution of queries on other tables in the database. While we, the users of SQL, must decide when and how indexes are created, we need not decide when they are used.

Creating Indexes

Each index applies to a single table and must also specify one or more columns in that table whose values should be indexed. To create an index, one uses SQL's **CREATE INDEX** statement. Although the SQL standard defines no common way to create indexes (in fact, it doesn't mention indexes at all), the general form of **CREATE INDEX** in most implementations is

```
CREATE INDEX <name>
    ON <table>(<columns>);
```

where **<name>** is a name for the new index, **<table>** identifies which table is to be indexed, and **<columns>** names the column or columns on which the index is to be based. For example, to create an index called **NAMES** on the `teacher_name` column of the **TEACHERS** table, one would type

```
CREATE INDEX NAMES
    ON TEACHERS(teacher_name);
```

A new table now exists, called **NAMES**, containing an index of the `teacher_name`s in **TEACHERS**. To get an idea of what this index table actually looks like, refer to Figure 11.1. As the figure shows, an index can be thought of as simply an ordered list of the values in the indexed column. Instead of the random record order of **TEACHERS**, the **NAMES** index orders the values of its indexed column in a specific way, e.g., in alphabetical order. Stored with each record in the index is an indication of where the record containing that value actually occurs in the table being indexed. For example, the first entry in the index table **NAMES** in Figure 11.1 contains the value **Dr. Cooke**, along with a "pointer" to where Dr. Cooke's record occurs in **TEACHERS**. The second index entry contains **Dr. Engle** and a pointer to Dr. Engle's record, and so on.

Now, each time a query is executed against **TEACHERS** that requires SQL to find a specific teacher's name, the index **NAMES** may be automatically consulted. Rather than exhaustively searching the unordered records in **TEACHERS**, a much faster search is made of the alphabetically ordered teacher names in the index **NAMES**. (It's much easier to locate a specific element in an ordered list than in a list with no order—compare the difficulty, for instance, of looking up someone's phone number in a normal telephone directory with that of looking up the same number in a telephone directory with randomly listed names.) Once the correct record in **NAMES** is located, it is a simple matter to follow that record's pointer to the desired record in **TEACHERS**. And to keep the index up to date, any new records added to **TEACHERS** are automatically added to **NAMES**, as well. (Note that with some systems, an additional command is required after creation of the index to allow its automatic use during execution of a query. One example of such a system is IBM's DB2.)

It is also possible to create indexes in which the values in the indexed columns are guaranteed to be unique. This is done by specifying the **UNIQUE** option when the index is created, like

```
CREATE UNIQUE INDEX UNAMES
    ON TEACHERS(teacher_name);
```

As before, an index table is created, containing ordered values of `teacher_name` and pointers back to the original records in **TEACHERS**. This time, however, all teacher names are required to be unique. Furthermore, if an attempt is made to add a new record to **TEACHERS** with a teacher name identical to one already found in the table, the addition will be rejected. (Note that if the **UNIQUE** option was specified for this column when the table was created, addition of a record with a duplicate value for that column will be rejected regardless of whether any index exists. As was mentioned in Chapter 7, many SQL systems currently support the **UNIQUE** option only on **CREATE INDEX** and not on the **CREATE TABLE** statement.)

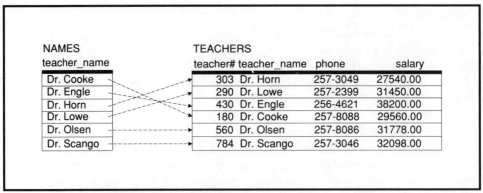

Figure 11.1 *An index on the* TEACHERS *table*

A note about implementation: the exact structure of index tables varies from one SQL implementation to another. Some may order indexed columns alphabetically while others use more complex techniques. Similarly, the index's pointers back to the main table may be implemented in a variety of ways. None of this is visible to a SQL user, however, since the index is automatically used by SQL whenever possible.

When To Create Indexes

Exactly which indexes you create should depend on what kinds of queries you plan to execute. If you will often be searching for teachers by name, then the creation of the **NAMES** index above would speed up these queries. For some kinds of queries, it may help to build indexes using more than one column. Suppose, for instance, that you often wished to access information about students by course number and section number. To help with this, you might create an index on **ENROLLS** called **CSECT** with

```
CREATE INDEX CSECT
    ON ENROLLS(course#, section#);
```

This creates an index like that described earlier, except that the index relies on two values to find each record in the indexed table. The **CSECT** index would speed up queries like

```
SELECT student_name
    FROM STUDENTS, ENROLLS
    WHERE course# = 450 AND
          section# = 1 AND
          STUDENTS.student# = ENROLLS.student#;
```

Note once again that the index is never explicitly mentioned in the query. SQL simply uses it whenever possible.

Perhaps the most important use of indexes is in speeding up the execution of joins. Joining two tables can be a very time consuming operation, especially if either or both of the tables are large. Joining more than two tables can sometimes be *very* slow, trying the patience of any user. If the columns being joined have previously had indexes constructed for them, execution of the join may be ten or even a hundred times faster.

As we have seen, joins most often occur on columns containing keys. We have often joined **STUDENTS** and **ENROLLS**, for instance, on the columns called **student#**. The **student#** column is the key to the records in **STUDENTS**, and therefore guarantees that each of those records is uniquely identifiable. In **ENROLLS**, on the other hand, **student#** is a foreign key, containing key values from another table. A query like

```
SELECT student_name, grade
    FROM STUDENTS, ENROLLS
    WHERE STUDENTS.student# = ENROLLS.student#;
```

would likely execute much faster if one or both of the join columns **STUDENTS.student#** and **ENROLLS.student#** were indexed. In other words, if you plan to perform many queries that join **STUDENTS** and **ENROLLS** on their **student#** columns, those queries would almost certainly execute faster if you first typed

```
CREATE INDEX SS#
    ON STUDENTS(student#);
```

and

```
CREATE INDEX ES#
    ON ENROLLS(student#);
```

The indexes **SS#** and **ES#** will be automatically used by SQL whenever possible.

Destroying Indexes

Just as indexes can be created, they can also be destroyed. As with tables and views, a variant of SQL's **DROP** statement is usually used. Its general form is

```
DROP INDEX <name>;
```

where **<name>** identifies the index to destroy. To destroy the **NAMES** index created above, for instance, you would type

```
DROP INDEX NAMES;
```

while the command to destroy the **CSECT** index is

```
DROP INDEX CSECT;
```

Using Multiple SQL Statements to Solve a Problem

Up to this point, all the examples shown have used only a single SQL statement. In real life, answering many interesting questions requires using multiple SQL statements, one after another. Combining several SQL statements can be very powerful, especially when performing analysis on the information stored in a relational database. While there are a number of questions that cannot be answered by a single SQL statement, there are very few that cannot be answered by the proper combination of SQL statements.

Suppose, for instance, that we want to learn which student has the lowest grade point average (GPA). We can list all students and their GPAs with

```
SELECT student_name,
       gpa = SUM(grade * num_credits) /
             SUM(num_credits)
   FROM STUDENTS S, ENROLLS E, COURSES C
   WHERE S.student# = E.student# AND
         C.course# = E.course#
   GROUP BY student_name;
```

We ourselves could then look through this list for the student (or students) with the lowest grade point average. As always, though, we want SQL to do our work for us, so this solution is not ideal.

Unfortunately, constructing a single SQL query which will find only those students with the lowest GPA is a difficult task. Being certain that the query is *correct*, especially if the database is so large that we can't easily check the results, is even more difficult. In many cases, it is easier and less error-prone to answer complex questions in more than one step, using several SQL statements.

To do this, we must first use **CREATE** to create a temporary table. This table will be used to hold partial results, produced in one step of the process, which can then be used as input to the next step. We may perform **SELECT**s and other operations on this temporary table, perhaps in combination with operations on other tables in the database. When the desired end results have been obtained, we will delete the temporary table.

For example, to solve the problem stated above—learning who has the lowest GPA—you might first create a temporary table called **GPAS** with

```
CREATE TABLE GPAS
    (student_name CHAR(18),
    gpa FLOAT);
```

Next, this table must be populated with records, each containing a student's name and his or her GPA. That information is exactly what the **SELECT** statement shown above returns, so using the **SELECT** option of the **INSERT** statement yields

```
INSERT INTO GPAS
    SELECT student_name,
           gpa = SUM(grade * num_credits) /
                 SUM(num_credits)
       FROM STUDENTS S, ENROLLS E, COURSES C
       WHERE S.student# = E.student# AND
             C.course# = E.course#
       GROUP BY student_name;
```

We now have a table called **GPAS** which, for each student, contains one record with that student's name and GPA. (Although not defined by the SQL standard, some systems allow a **SELECT** to be part of the **CREATE TABLE** statement. This effectively allows the two previous queries to be combined into a single query.) Even though we know that this table is merely temporary, to SQL it is a table like any other.

You can now easily determine which student has the lowest GPA by querying the **GPA** table with

```
SELECT student_name, gpa
    FROM GPAS
    WHERE gpa IN
            (SELECT MIN(gpa)
                FROM GPAS);
```

The result of this query is the name and GPA of the student or students with the lowest grade point average.

To complete the process, the temporary table should be destroyed. While not strictly required, removal of the table is a good idea, since it consumes space in the database. Like all tables, **GPA** can be destroyed with

DROP TABLE GPA;

For many complex questions, it may be possible to construct a single query which produces an answer. Not infrequently, however, creating a temporary table, filling it with appropriate records, and querying that table is much simpler than devising a single complex query against existing tables. As a general rule, if a simple solution gives the same results as a more complex one, the simple solution is better.

Example: using a temporary table

• *Problem*

Which student has the lowest GPA?

• *Query Diagram (Creating the Temporary Table)*

GPAS	
student_name	CHAR(18)
gpa	FLOAT

• *SQL (Creating the Temporary Table)*

```
CREATE TABLE GPAS
    (student_name CHAR(18),
     gpa FLOAT);
```

• Query Diagram (Populating the Temporary Table)

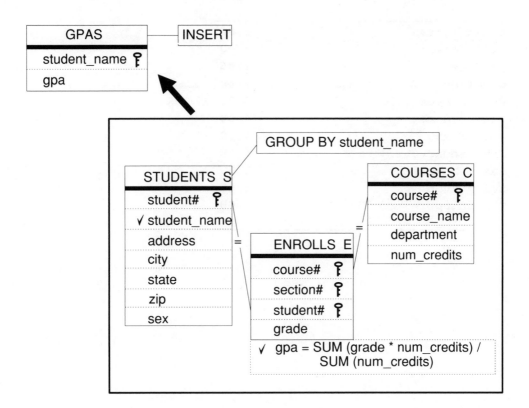

• SQL (Populating the Temporary Table)

```
INSERT INTO GPAS
    SELECT student_name,
           gpa = SUM(grade * num_credits) /
                 SUM(num_credits)
        FROM STUDENTS S, ENROLLS E, COURSES C
        WHERE S.student# = E.student# AND
              C.course# = E.course#
        GROUP BY student_name;
```

• Results (Contents of the Temporary Table)

student_name	gpa
Allen Thomas	1.00
Bill Jones	2.00
Bob Dawson	1.86
Carol Dean	1.80
Howard Mansfield	3.00
Janet Thomas	4.00
Joe Adams	4.00
John Anderson	4.00
Susan Powell	3.00
Susan Pugh	2.00
Val Shipp	3.00

• *Query Diagram (Querying the Temporary Table)*

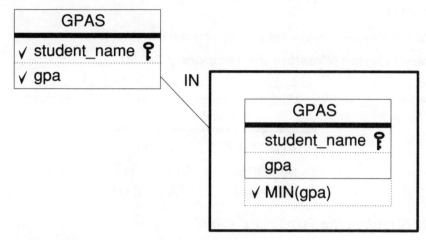

• *SQL (Querying the Temporary Table)*

```
SELECT student_name, gpa
    FROM GPAS
    WHERE gpa IN
        (SELECT MIN(gpa)
            FROM GPAS);
```

• *Results*

student_name	gpa
Allen Thomas	1.00

• *Query Diagram (Dropping the Temporary Table)*

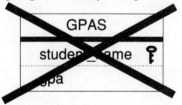

• *SQL (Dropping the Temporary Table)*

```
DROP TABLE GPAS;
```

Example: using a temporary table

• Problem

Find the teacher who, on the average, gives the highest grades.

• Query Diagram (Creating the Temporary Table)

TEMP	
avg_grade	FLOAT
students	SMALLINT
teacher#	SMALLINT

• SQL (Creating the Temporary Table)

```
CREATE TABLE TEMP
    (avg_grade FLOAT,
     students SMALLINT,
     teacher# SMALLINT);
```

• *Query Diagram (Populating the Temporary Table)*

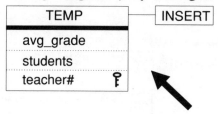

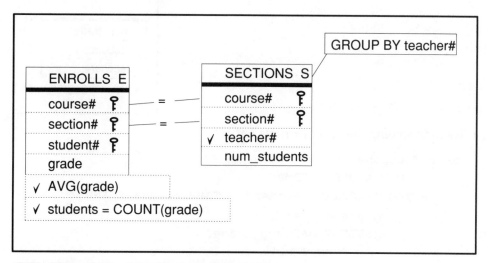

• *SQL (Populating the Temporary Table)*

```
INSERT INTO TEMP
    SELECT avg_grade = AVG(grade),
           students = COUNT(grade), teacher#
        FROM ENROLLS E, SECTIONS S
        WHERE S.course# = E.course# AND
              E.section# = S.section#
        GROUP BY teacher#;
```

• *Results (Contents of the Temporary Table)*

avg_grade	students	teacher#
3.33	3	180
2.67	6	290
3.00	2	303
3.00	3	430
3.00	1	560
1.50	2	784

• Query Diagram (Querying the Temporary Table)

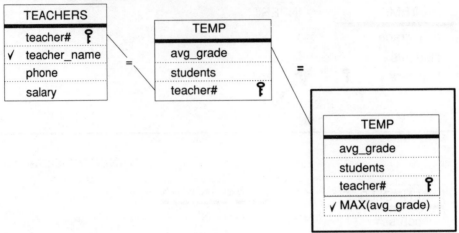

• SQL (Querying the Temporary Table)

```
SELECT teacher_name
    FROM TEACHERS, TEMP
    WHERE TEACHERS.teacher# = TEMP.teacher# AND
        avg_grade =
        (SELECT MAX(avg_grade)
            FROM TEMP);
```

• Results

```
teacher_name
```
_____

```
Dr. Cooke
```
_____

• Query Diagram (Dropping the Temporary Table)

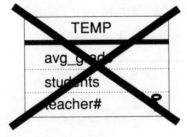

• SQL (Dropping the Temporary Table)

```
DROP TABLE TEMP;
```

Example: using a temporary table

• *Problem*

Find the department with the most women students.

• *Query Diagram (Creating the Temporary Table)*

TEMPW	
department	CHAR(16)
number	SMALLINT

• *SQL (Creating the Temporary Table)*

```
CREATE TABLE TEMPW
        (department CHAR(20),
         number     SMALLINT);
```

• *Query Diagram (Populating the Temporary Table)*

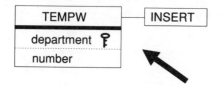

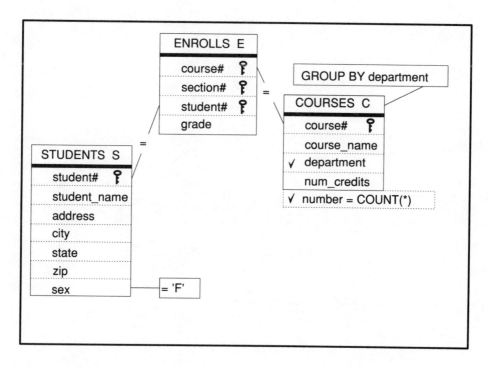

• SQL (Populating the Temporary Table)

```
INSERT INTO TEMPW
    SELECT department, number = COUNT(*)
    FROM COURSES C, ENROLLS E, STUDENTS S
    WHERE sex = 'F' AND
        C.course# = E.course# AND
        S.student# = E.student#
    GROUP BY department;
```

• Results (Contents of the Temporary Table)

department	number
Computer Science	1
History	2
Math	4

• Query Diagram (Querying the Temporary Table)

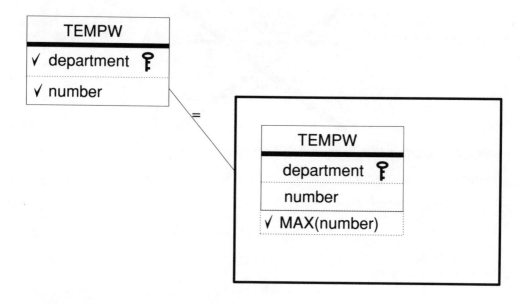

• SQL (Querying the Temporary Table)

```
SELECT department, number
     FROM TEMPW
     WHERE number =
             (SELECT MAX(number)
                 FROM TEMPW);
```

• Results

department	number
Math	4

• Query Diagram (Dropping the Temporary Table)

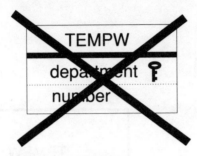

• SQL (Dropping the Temporary Table)

```
DROP TABLE TEMPW;
```

Unions

Although seldom used, SQL allows a user to combine the results of queries with a *union*. Two queries can have their results grouped together simply by typing the two queries with the word **UNION** between them. The result of executing a union is just a list containing the results of both queries.

For example, we could list the names and numbers of all students and all teachers with

```
SELECT number = student#, name = student_name
    FROM STUDENTS
UNION
SELECT teacher#, teacher_name
    FROM TEACHERS;
```

The result of this query is a single table whose records consist of records containing either student number and name pairs or teacher number and name pairs. Although all the results of both **SELECT**s will appear, they may appear in any order.

Unions can only be used when the results of the two queries have exactly the same types. In other words, both must return the same number of columns, and those columns must contain the same type and length of data. In the example above, for instance, both **SELECT**s return two identical columns of types **CHAR(18)** and **SMALLINT**.

Example: using a union

• Problem

List the names and numbers of all students and all teachers.

• Query Diagram

TEACHERS
✓ teacher# ☍
✓ teacher_name
phone
salary

UNION

STUDENTS
✓ student# ☍
✓ student_name
address
city
state
zip
sex

• SQL

```
SELECT number = student#, name = student_name
    FROM STUDENTS
UNION
SELECT teacher#, teacher_name
    FROM TEACHERS;
```

• Results

```
number name
```

number	name
148	Susan Powell
180	Dr. Cooke
210	Bob Dawson
290	Dr. Lowe
298	Howard Mansfield
303	Dr. Horn
348	Susan Pugh
349	Joe Adams
354	Janet Ladd
410	Bill Jones
430	Dr. Engle
473	Carol Dean
548	Allen Thomas
558	Val Shipp
560	Dr. Olsen
649	John Anderson
654	Janet Thomas
784	Dr. Scango

Joining a Table With Itself

In Chapter 5, we saw how the information stored in two or more different tables could be accessed at once via joins. While not often done, it is also possible to join a table with itself. Suppose, for example, that we want to see a list of all teacher names and salaries where, for each teacher, we also list the names and salaries of every teacher who earns more. All of this information is contained within the **TEACHERS** table, so a join with another table is not required. Nevertheless, there is no simple query without a join that can produce the desired results. A join must be used, but this time, the **TEACHERS** table must be joined with itself.

Before showing the required SQL query, one more new idea must be introduced: joins using an operator other than =. Although all joins seen in this book so far compare columns in two tables for equality, it is also possible to use operators like < and > for these comparisons. To imagine how this works, remember the results of a join with no **WHERE** clause: a list of all possible combinations of records from the two tables. When a **WHERE** clause is added, only those records that meet its conditions are selected from this large table. Up to now, this condition has always been that particular fields from the two tables' columns contain the same value, i.e., that they are equal. It is also possible to select from the results of the **WHERE**-less join records in which one of those values is less than the other, or greater than, or simply different, i.e., not equal. While joins that test for equality are much more common, some kinds of questions (such as the one asked above) need to use other tests.

Back to the original problem: generating a list of all teacher names and salaries which, for each teacher, includes a list of the names and salaries of all teachers who earn more. This can be accomplished with

```
SELECT lower_paid = T1.teacher_name,
       lower_salary = T1.salary,
       higher_paid = T2.teacher_name,
       higher_salary = T2.salary
   FROM TEACHERS T1, TEACHERS T2
   WHERE T1.salary < T2.salary
   ORDER BY 1;
```

Because we want to compare values drawn from the same column of the same table, aliases must be used to correctly formulate this query. Those aliases, **T1** and **T2**, assign two different names to the **TEACHERS** table, allowing us to correctly express the condition in the **WHERE** clause. If the **WHERE** clause were not present, this query would result in a listing of every teacher's name and salary paired with the name and salary of every other teacher. With the **WHERE** clause, only those records in which one salary column is less than the other will be selected.

The result of this query is a four-column list. The first two columns, **lower_paid** and **lower_salary**, contain the names and salaries of the lower paid teachers. Each teacher's name and salary will appear in this column once for every teacher who earns more than he or she does. The columns on the right hand side of the list are named **higher_paid** and **higher_salary**. For each teacher, these two columns will contain the names and salaries of every other teacher who is better paid. The entire list is ordered alphabetically by the names of the lower paid teachers.

Example: joining a table with itself

• *Problem*

For every teacher, list the names and salaries of teachers who earn more.

• *Query Diagram*

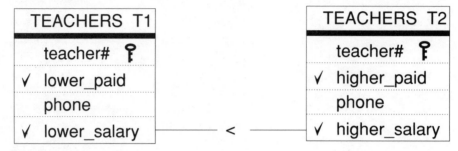

•*SQL*

```
SELECT lower_paid = T1.teacher_name,
       lower_salary = T1.salary,
       higher_paid = T2.teacher_name,
       higher_salary = T2.salary
   FROM TEACHERS T1, TEACHERS T2
   WHERE T1.salary  < T2.salary
   ORDER BY 1;
```

• Results

lower_paid	lower_salary	higher_paid	higher_salary
Dr. Cooke	29560.00	Dr. Olsen	31778.00
Dr. Cooke	29560.00	Dr. Lowe	31450.00
Dr. Cooke	29560.00	Dr. Scango	32098.00
Dr. Cooke	29560.00	Dr. Engle	38200.00
Dr. Horn	27540.00	Dr. Engle	38200.00
Dr. Horn	27540.00	Dr. Olsen	31778.00
Dr. Horn	27540.00	Dr. Lowe	31450.00
Dr. Horn	27540.00	Dr. Cooke	29560.00
Dr. Horn	27540.00	Dr. Scango	32098.00
Dr. Lowe	31450.00	Dr. Olsen	31778.00
Dr. Lowe	31450.00	Dr. Engle	38200.00
Dr. Lowe	31450.00	Dr. Scango	32098.00
Dr. Olsen	31778.00	Dr. Engle	38200.00
Dr. Olsen	31778.00	Dr. Scango	32098.00
Dr. Scango	32098.00	Dr. Engle	38200.00

Appendix A: The Example Database

ENROLLS

course#	section#	student#	grade
730	1	148	3
450	2	210	3
730	1	210	1
290	1	298	3
480	2	298	3
730	1	348	2
290	1	349	4
480	1	358	4
480	1	410	2
450	1	473	2
730	1	473	3
480	2	473	0
290	1	548	2
730	1	558	3
730	1	649	4
480	1	649	4
450	1	654	4
450	2	548	

TEACHERS

teacher#	teacher_name	phone	salary
303	Dr. Horn	257-3049	27540.00
290	Dr. Lowe	257-2390	31450.00
430	Dr. Engle	256-4621	38200.00
180	Dr. Cooke	257-8088	29560.00
560	Dr. Olsen	257-8086	31778.00
784	Dr. Scango	257-3046	32098.00

COURSES

course#	course_name	department	num_credits
450	Western Civilization	History	3
730	Calculus IV	Math	4
290	English Composition	English	3
480	Compiler Writing	Computer Science	3

SECTIONS

section#	teacher#	course#	num_students
1	303	450	2
1	290	730	6
1	430	290	3
1	180	480	3
2	560	450	2
2	784	480	2

STUDENTS

student#	student_name	address	zip	city	state	sex
148	Susan Powell	534 East River Dr.	19041	Haverford	PA	F
210	Bob Dawson	120 South Jefferson	02891	Newport	RI	M
298	Howard Mansfield	290 Wynkoop Drive	22180	Vienna	VA	M
348	Susan Pugh	534 East Hampton Dr.	06107	Hartford	CN	F
349	Joe Adams	473 Emmerson Street	19702	Newark	DE	M
354	Janet Ladd	441 10th Street	18073	Pennsburg	PA	F
410	Bill Jones	120 South Harrison	92660	Newport	CA	M
473	Carol Dean	983 Park Avenue	02169	Boston	MA	F
548	Allen Thomas	238 West Ox Road	60624	Chicago	IL	M
558	Val Shipp	238 Westport Road	60556	Chicago	IL	F
649	John Anderson	473 Emmory Street	10008	New York	NY	M
654	Janet Thomas	441 6th Street	16510	Erie	PA	F

Appendix B: List of Examples

1   Introducing SQL

2   Elements of the Language

3   Retrieving Data From a Table: The SELECT Statement

4   More On SELECT

5   Retrieving Data From Several Tables: Joins

6   Queries Within Queries: Subqueries

7   Creating and Destroying Tables

8   Adding, Modifying, and Deleting Records

9   Views

10   Granting and Revoking Privileges

11   Advanced Topics

Index

A

adding records to a table
> using SELECT to specify values, 165
> with values for all columns, 160
> with values only for some columns, 161

adding records to a view, 192
aggregates, 59
aliases, 102
ALL
> with GRANT, 203
> with subqueries, 131

ALTER, 149
AND, 27
ANSI SQL, 8
ANY, 131
arithmetic operations in queries, 56
ASC, 50
AVG, 66
averaging a column's values, 66

B

base table, 180
BETWEEN and NOT BETWEEN, 35

C

changing a table's structure, 149
CHAR, *see* CHARACTER
CHARACTER, 9
CHECK option, in views, 192
Codd, E.F., 2
columns, 2
correlated subqueries, 138
correlation names, *see* aliases
COUNT, 68
counting records in a table, 68
CREATE INDEX, 221
CREATE TABLE, 148
CREATE VIEW, 180
creating indexes, 221